"*The Seven Women Project* is a fun, insightful look at the constant tug-of-war of fashion and fancy inside us all. I teeter-totter between being a Hanna/Zoë and a Gwen. When Gwen gets her way and I put on the heels and the fantastic dress, we have a blast. Then she very quickly sends me back to Hanna (hungover) and Zoë (to yoga to clean my system back out.) It's a vicious cycle and it actually works pretty well!"

Laura McCreary, Comedy Writer

"*The Seven Women Project* is a brilliant, creative piece of work that captures and honors the depth and richness in each of us. This book is fun, entertaining, and yes, even enlightening. It allowed me to celebrate my personal journey and highlighted the "shadow side." Hats off to Karen and Meredith!"

Bambi McCullough, CEO Chrysalis Partners
(Not related!)

"Funny, poignant and very entertaining, this book celebrates the multi-faceted nature of women. It gives new meaning to the belief that "we are not alone"! *The Seven Women Project* has provided me with a better understanding of myself, and just as important, more insight into the women whose paths cross mine on a daily basis."

Teri Battaglieri, Special Assistant to the
Director of the Michigan Teacher's Association

"Reading *The Seven Woman Project* inspired me to reclaim and celebrate parts of myself that I had forgotten or misunderstood. It deepened my appreciation for the variety of all the special women in my life and the way we continuously change and re-invent ourselves."

Desirée Rumbaugh, Certified Anusara Yoga Instructor

"Women who want to be leaders today often buy into the wrong definition of leadership. It is filled with masculine behavior and imagery. In reality, the evolving and new definition of leadership encompasses both masculine and feminine traits. As women, we no longer need to check our feminine selves at the business door. Karen and Meredith McCullough do a wonderful job capturing this in Gwen. Your inner Gwen puts this all in perspective. Allow her vulnerability, femininity, and receptivity guide you as a leader in the 21st century."

Laura Lopez, author: The Connected and Committed Leader: Lessons from Home, Results at Work.

"This amazing mother-daughter team has taken the characteristics of the modern woman and defined them out loud and with humor for all of us to enjoy. They provide a platform for us to look within and re-imagine who we can be as our best selves. As an entrepreneur, I for one will be tapping my inner-Donna moving forward!"

Malissa McLeod
Owner and Designer, Malissa McLeod Interiors

"After reading *The Seven Women Project* I reorganized my closet into seven sections. (Okay, six because Hanna got a drawer). My husband was nice enough to agree to use the closet in the guest room. I loved the book!"

Kim Healy, CEO Love Handle Handbags

"I have always been such a "Kate"! But learned from *The Seven Women Project* that I am also "Hanna" and "Donna," and now is the time to let my "Sophia" out. Since learning about the seven women, I have been able to use this within my own interior design business by identifying who each of my clients are, and expressing that style through their homes."

Karen Davis, CEO Karen Davis Design

"*The Seven Women Project* is charming, witty, and inspiring. It embraces the existence (and encourages the exploration) of the multiple dimensions and aspects of ourselves as women, not to mention offers some great fashion advice. As I read it, I found myself touched by each woman and received several nuggets of wisdom and guidance from each one, while affirming that these insights were already inside of me, as well as parts of each of these women. It is truly empowering and uplifting, and a must-read for women of all ages!"

Ren Resch, Consultant, Yoga and Meditation Instructor, and Explorer Extraordinaire

"Karen McCullough and Meredith McCullough help us to gain understanding and acceptance of our own complexities. No matter which of the seven women we mainly identify with, we know we have the strength and backup from the other women within ourselves. Keep this book within reach, like a good friend, there are days when you need the support it gives you."

Kim Zeiner , Senior Account Manager

"This is the best book for women I have ever read. Ok, it's the only book for women I have ever read but it's still great! Good insights and I learned a lot about how the female mind works. Well done!"

Garrison Wynn
Professional Speaker, Author: The Real Truth About Success

"*The Seven Women Project* is full of personality and fun. While reading the book I was hoping Karen and Meredith would come over and coach the team of women within me, but by the end, I had taken some notes and created a plan that I hope to execute on my own. The Seven Women Project is a great resource and even a guide for balance in our lives. This book acknowledges that women are called to wear many hats, the trick is knowing when to switch over...and then wearing the right hat with style!"

Aurelie Gallagher Krauss
CEO Irish Eyes Design (and mother of three)

The Seven Women Project
*Your Personal Guides to Success
in Work, Play and Dress*

Karen McCullough
Meredith McCullough

the
seven
WOMEN
project

*Your
Personal Guides
to Success
in Work, Play
and Dress*

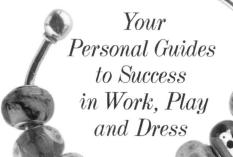

Karen McCullough & Meredith McCullough

The Seven Women Project
Your Personal Guides to Success in Work, Play and Dress

Willard St. Publishers
Houston, TX

By Karen McCullough and Meredith McCullough
All Rights Reserved ©2010 by Karen McCullough

Published by Willard St. Publishers
Printed in the United States of America
thesevenwomenproject.com

Author:	Karen McCullough
	Meredith McCullough
Book and Cover Design:	Mike Svat
Illustrations:	Shyama Golden

13-digit ISBN: 978-0-9843106-6-1
9-digit ISBN: 0-9843106-6-5
Library of Congress Control Number: 2010921762

1. Self-help -- Psychology 2. Women -- Success
First Edition: March 2010

Willard St. Publishers books are available at special quantity discounts to use as premiums and sales promotions, or for use in corporate trainings or as conference materials.

For more information, please contact Director of Special Sales, Willard St. Publishers, 1302 Waugh Dr. #344, Houston, TX 77019.

All websites were validated February, 2010.

For Rose.
March 19, 1911 - June 8, 2009

A pioneer working woman, amazing cook, feisty Italian,
and a classic dresser well into her 90s,
Rose was quite remarkable in her own right …
… as well as mother, grandmother, and nana to three
generations of fabulous women.
She is loved and missed.

Contents

"Who am I to be brilliant, gorgeous, talented, fabulous? Actually, who are you not to be? ... We are all meant to shine ... It's not just in some of us; it's in everyone. And as we let our own light shine, we unconsciously give other people permission to do the same." [1]

Marianne Williamson
A Return To Love:
Reflections on the Principles
of A Course in Miracles

"Everyone has split personalities. You can be strong and vulnerable. Me? I have like five or six. There are many sides to me."

Pink

INTRODUCTION

Welcome to *The Seven Women Project*. We are honored to have the opportunity to share our work with you, and we invite you to participate in our big revelation: we are not alone. Inside every woman there are seven women. Seven extraordinary women, each one waiting, with eager anticipation, to be recognized, called upon, shared ... and dressed.

Our path toward this auspicious discovery began ten years ago as a simple conversation between mother and daughter. Since those kinds of conversations are never really quite so simple, it is no wonder that what emerged was a full-blown adventure.

When we first started this project, we were aiming to tell Karen's story, and the stories that she had heard from behind the dressing room doors during her time as a local fashion guru in Houston, Texas. We thought that we were telling a story about fashion, about style, and about how to break out of our daily dressing ruts to literally "try on" something new. It turned out that dressing was only part of the equation. *The Seven Women Project* is about more, much more.

What has followed has been a decade of creative wrangling and spirited collaboration that has meant countless hours sifting through memories, recalling experiences, and retelling what we have seen and heard out there, beyond the dressing room doors...with a little self-reflection and personal growth thrown in to the mix.

Ten years into the project and we still struggle to define our partnership and ourselves. We do not pretend to be psychologists or personality experts. We are a mother-daughter dynamic duo, and together we have run the duo gamut: motivational speaker and government consultant; business owner and international volunteer; jazzercise fanatic and yoga instructor. We are dog-walker and marathon runner; fashionista and feminista; cool kid and pop-culture nerd; Baby Boomer and Gen X'er. We are mother, daughters, sisters and friends. And we are women.

In the end, this what *The Seven Women Project* is really about. It is a story about women and how we connect, grow, and shine as we strive to bring out our best and truest selves. This work is our heartfelt celebration. It is celebration of women and of each of us as women – with all our complexities and contradictions, our talents and our values, our passion and our vision. It is a celebration of the abundant reserve of strength, ingenuity, and know-how that we each have inside of us, with a playful nudge reminding us to let it all out.

Through this process we have come to see women as dynamic, creative, intelligent, spiritual, sensual, mysterious, loving, generous, and playful beings. Women are multi-dimensional, and as women we are asked to play multiple roles and to be many things to many different people. Sometimes we feel overwhelmed. Sometimes we feel misunderstood. Sometimes we feel alone. And sometimes, just sometimes, we tend to forget how wondrous we really are.

Our challenge with this book is to bring out the "more" in women – more life, more diversity, more possibility, and yes, more style. We believe that whether facing life's challenges or experiencing the best of times, women at any age have the capacity to look deeper into who they already are, get inspired, and call into action some previously un-tapped aspects of their best, most authentic selves.

    We hope that the characters, stories, lists, tips, and ideas contained in *The Seven Women Project* will serve to spark your already brilliant store of creative energy, and unleash your confidence to let go and trust. Trust your gut, trust your heart, and (at times) your mother (She made me say it). Be-cause ultimately, we know that we are not alone. Inside each of us there is a team, an entire community of women to coach us, guide us, and make us look absolutely gorgeous along our way.

"Success is easy.
It just takes all you've got."

Karen McCullough

CHAPTER ONE

The Beginning

Women of all generations have been on my radar for a long time. As a fashion buyer and owner of boutique clothing stores, I have dressed them. As a boss and co-worker, I have mentored them. As a speaker, consultant and coach, I have listened to and encouraged them. As a daughter, sister, mother, and friend, I have been there for them, and they have been there for me.

I have had the opportunity to work with women in all kinds of settings – from oil refineries in Texas City, Texas to luxury spas in Phoenix, Arizona. I've met with women's professional groups from coast to coast and presented to CEOs, educators, auditors, probation officers, and engineers. All these experiences and the relationships I've formed over the years have shaped who I am today and how I see women. Each encounter has contributed to my own perspective on women – the challenges we have faced and the successes we have achieved.

I have heard some amazing stories and met some incredible people, but when you get right down to it, for me, it's always been about … the clothes. I just can't help it. I got my training behind the dressing room door and it stuck with me. I have a passion for fashion, and I've had it for as long as I can remember.

The Early Years

My sisters tell me it was only a year or two after I was born that our mother Rose took a full-time job in downtown Cleveland, Ohio at Sterling Linder. These were the golden years of the department store and Sterling Linder did it all. Snazzy elevator attendants shuttled customers from floor to floor. Glamorous window displays stopped busy pedestrians in their tracks. And at Christmas time, the store boasted that it had "the world's biggest" indoor tree.

My mother was hired as the Credit Manager. She made $50 a week.

I did not recognize at the time just how smart and brave my mother was. This was the 1950s and traditional womens' roles were limited. Most of the women in our Little Italy neighborhood created a life around care of the home and family. My mother loved us, but she needed to get out and engage with the rest of the world. When she left our apartment every morning and walked down Murray Hill to take the train to the city, she was doing something truly exceptional.

Yet for all her strength, my mother had pangs of guilt about leaving me, her youngest, at home all day with my Italian-speaking grandmother. Her solution was to bring me to work with her as often as possible, and she used some big-time pull to sneak me into the department store system at an early age.

When I was five, she convinced the buyer in the Children's Wear Department to use me in the store fashion shows. At Christmas time, I was one of Santa's elves. And when I was 14, they had me working (we called it "volunteering") in the sub-basement, receiving and tagging garments before they hit the floor.

My big break came at 16, when they assigned me to

the Junior Miss Department, or as I liked to call it, "Heaven." There, I fell in love with my first label, Jonathan Logan, the Isaac Mizrahi of the times. Girls came in droves to try on these simple, but sharp dresses and I was more than happy to help them spend, spend, spend.

No doubt about it. Retail is in my blood.

Living the American Dream

By the time I was 30, I had done everything I was supposed to do. I went to college to study something practical, married my boyfriend from freshman year, and soon started a family of my own with two great kids and a dog. Growing up in Little Italy, my childhood fantasy was to live in nearby Chagrin Falls, the "Preppy Capitol of the World." Instead, I found myself packing for a move south to the booming oil "town" of Houston, Texas to follow my husband's burgeoning career. I became a stay-at-home mom, and to pass the time I built an active volunteer-life at my kids' school. I took gourmet-cooking classes and taught myself to weave. And, still, I was bored.

I needed more. So, I did what any young woman in my situation would do: I started a business.

With little more than enthusiasm and good intentions, I opened a preppy clothing store in the far west suburbs of Houston. Back then, that little store was pure magic. As crazy as it sounds, business exploded into success from the get-go. It became a neighborhood hot spot and clothing seemed to fly off the racks. We made it look easy, and at the time it was.

I had come a long way from the Junior Miss Department. Now, like my mother did with me, I went to the store with my children in tow.

As it often happens in these fabulous success stories, one thing leads to another. Sometimes it's all about being at the right place at the right time – and Houston in the early 1980s was definitely that right place for a small business owner like myself. Soon I had opened a second store in a different part of town, then a third and a fourth. My 400-square-foot neighborhood shop was transformed into a small chain with multiple locations in a thriving, modern metropolitan city.

Owning and operating a retail store made my dream come true, and I felt like I was in a real-life fairy tale.

Girl Interrupting

Hold on. Hold on. Before we get too far here, I think we need to clear the air just a bit. Did we say that this is Karen's story? Well, maybe technically, but I think there is a little bit more to tell.

They say that behind every man there is a successful woman. The part that seems to get left out, however, is that behind every successful woman is ... well, her daughter. Who else? Who else do you think would be there to fill the role of confidant, assistant and maybe, on occasion, dress-up doll? If you don't believe me, ask Chelsea Clinton.

As Karen's daughter, I can assure you that I was there from the beginning. Okay, maybe not the very beginning. Obviously, I was not there for that whole glammed-up department store bit, but I was there when she decided it would be a cool idea to open a little local clothing store ... in our spare bedroom. Did she tell you it started in our house? That is, until the nice constable knocked on the door and told her that she needed a permit to operate a retail establishment and suggested that she find some actual commercial space to rent. She always leaves that part out.

Cheers!

My kids used to compare working at the front counter of my
store to bartending. Women would come in and I would
wipe down the counter, pop open a dressing room, and listen.
I got quite an earful.

I listened to them talk about their jobs, families, and
the kids' soccer games. They told me about annoying cowork-
ers and impossible bosses, about their need to get promoted,
and move up into management roles. I heard about their
dates, their dreams, and their disasters. They bragged about
their accomplishments and cried about their defeats.

Behind those dressing room doors, women felt safe
enough to unload their deepest concerns and woes – relationship woes, fashion woes, and I-hate-my-body woes. At times
it felt like a confessional. Women would come in and tell all.
"I hate my job!" "My kids drive me crazy!" "I have nothing
to wear!" "I can't do it all!" "My thighs are too lumpy!" "My
legs are too short!" "My boobs are too big!"

But instead of a drink or an act of contrition, we
drowned their sorrows in clothes, purses, and shoulder pads
(lots and lots of shoulder pads). When "Happy Hour" was
over, they left the dressing rooms carrying piles of clothes,
scarves, accessories, and stacks of shoes. Arms full, they
marched right over to the checkout, buzzing with excitement
over their new purchases. Business was good.

As it turns out, I was getting more from those hours
in the back of the store than a thriving business. Women are
natural communicators, and as they spoke of their lives filled
with passion and disappointment, I subconsciously began to
collect data and make observations. It was from this vantage
point that I watched and experienced women over the next 20
years. All of this has come together to form the foundation for
this book. It's been a decade in the writing, and a lifetime in

the making.

We Are Family

"The store" as we called it, became part of our family identity. When my older cousins graduated from college, one-by-one they came down to Texas from Ohio to find themselves. And they found themselves all right. One found herself as a store manager, one as an accountant specializing in retail, one as a clothing manufacturer, and one as a showroom representative. The whole family found a niche in or around the store. Yes, retail must have certainly been in our blood, but to tell you the truth, I don't think it was ever really for me. And I resisted it, as much as I could.

True, I worked at the store for as long as I can remember. When it was the little shop on the corner (right after it moved out of the house), I walked there from the elementary school, and then later from middle and high school. When I was 12, I made ribbon-braided hair clips in the colors of the various Texas sororities to sell for pocket change and invented store jingles for the fifth grade talent show.

As I got older I was put in charge of bulk mailing all the store's advertising materials. Older still, I ran the back room – accepting COD packages from UPS, ripping open the boxes, and tagging all the goods. This was not Sterling Linder. The promotions were not glamorous. But I was featured (with really bad hair) in a couple of pretty cheesy ads. Not that I liked it or anything. Right?

I preferred those behind-the-scene duties to actually being on the selling floor. I mean, sure I could work a cash register without batting an eye, even when the computers were rolled in and confounded everyone.

While my mom was in the dressing rooms, I would lurk around and make sure that the racks were all organized – in size order, from the darkest to brightest colors. It's not that I was an ugly girl (I like to think I was actually quite popular in the "Sixteen Candles"-King-of-the, uh - nerds, kind of way). I just resisted the hype. Most girls my age would have killed to have a run of those stores. I just wanted to make sure they were running properly.

Dressing for Success – The Rise of the Great White Blouse

When it came to developing the look and feel of my first store, I turned to my new fashion hero for inspiration. At that time, Ralph Lauren had his hand on the pulse of American style. Ultimately, the rapid success of the store was a winning combination that was one part booming economy; one part fairy tale … and one part "Ralph."

In the early days, the store stayed true to the side of Ralph that embodied Classic Americana. As the 1980s swept through the city, however, the economic landscape started to shift. More and more of my customers were entering the workforce, and Houston women began to trade in their country, matchy-matchy outfits and turquoise broaches for pinstripes and pearls. Suburban life became less of a costume party – with serape blanket wrap skirts, studded blouses, fringed leather vests and suede jeans – and more of an office party. Image and perception took on unprecedented relevance. Whether they were going to work in a corporate office or opening their own businesses, my customers needed to develop a more professional look. They needed to be taken seriously and they embraced the more conservative side of Ralph with his homage to the classics, dressing smart in a great white blouse, pencil skirt, and anything cashmere.

I came up with a new store concept and a revised brand, tapping into the classics to resonate with my new generation of customers. To help us get clear on who we were and who we wanted to be, I created in my mind's eye the "perfect" customer for the store. It was no *Weird Science* experiment, but a brand development exercise. Either way, the first of the seven women was born. I named this ideal woman Kate – Classic and Classy Kate. Even in this early incarnation, Classic Kate was serious about getting ahead. She was a professional, stylish woman who participated in high-level meetings and felt good about herself. She was promoted into leadership roles and was destined to rise to CEO.

I liked and admired Kate and I was happy to buy for her. Every item we brought into the store had to pass the "Kate standard": conformity, clean lines, professional, and always appropriate. Year after year I sold fabulous black and gray pinstripes with dozens of great looking white blouses. Year after year my formula worked. My customers looked professional. They knew they looked great. And they met success head on.

What Would Kate Do?

If I were Jan Brady, Kate would have been my Marcia. I mean, really. That's all I ever heard, Kate, Kate, Kate! Whatever.

When I went off to college, I specifically sought out a "Kate"-free zone. No sororities. No dress code. All I needed was a good school newspaper, some intramural sports and, perhaps most importantly, to be at least a plane-ride away from the great state of Texas.

Reluctantly, I came home to help my mom with an in-store fashion show. It was supposed to highlight girls my age and what we were wearing in school. The scene was a college football game, and the ladies in the store wanted to know what I would wear. What I would wear? Really? I went to Notre Dame. But I guess jeans and a bootleg football t-shirt were not fashion show material, even with "real women on the runway."

I'm not going to say I hated it, but in true Gen X fashion, I did roll my eyes a lot. Can you blame me? Don't answer that.

Change is Good, You Go First

As the years passed, the same boredom I had when I was a stay-at-home mom reemerged; this time, I was bored with Kate. The passion and excitement of the early years of the store was gone. In my effort to stay true to my brand, I had created perfect Kate clones, and I was bored with the piles of great white blouses and the "keeping-it-together" look. I knew that there was more to these exciting women who were our customers, and it felt like I was down playing their individuality as I suited them up for work year after year.

I longed for something new. I longed for a change, some variety. I soon got what I wished for…I should have been more specific.

Then the 1990s arrived. Young software developers on the West Coast began making their mark, and it wasn't only with computer programs. Innovators like Bill Gates believed that his employees would work better if they were comfortable and relaxed, and casual work dress emerged. It didn't take long before the idea exploded into the biggest anti-fashion phenomenon our culture has ever seen.

Human resource departments jumped in on the action and offered casual dress as a perk. They allowed their employees to wear jeans, khakis, polo shirts, and sweaters to celebrate the end of the work week. Casual Friday became the norm in mainstream corporate America, and workers were onboard.

It didn't take long for Casual Friday to become "Casual Everyday." As the trend spread to the rest of the week, the deterioration of corporate style started to creep in. If workers wore casual clothes on Monday, Tuesday, Wednesday, and Thursday, then what made Friday special? People started digging way back into their closets for the Saturday stuff, like leggings, oversized tees, and flip-flops. "Oh, it's Friday," they said, "I'd better wear something more casual than I wore all week. Hmm, I mowed the yard in this. Perfect!"

My smart, stylish, exciting customers started dressing down, trading in their zippers for elastic, their gabardines for knits, their fitted, crisp white blouses for oversized tees. Women were giving up their power suits for baggy clothes and for some women there was no turning back. I had wanted change, but this wasn't what I had in mind. It was too depressing to watch.

The End of a Dream

Within a few years, business was down. Women stopped caring about fashion and the fashion rules. They wore white after Labor Day! They stopped ironing. They packed up their suits and their heels, threw out their pantyhose and got comfortable. I was feeling trapped in a business that was quickly becoming obsolete. I loved retail and had thought I would be in it until I died. But at this rate, it seemed like that might only be another few months.

I was growing increasingly anxious, and in my depressed state no one wanted to be around me. I constantly worried about open invoices, overdue sales taxes, payroll and markdowns… oh, those markdowns! I was stressed out, emotionally empty, and ready to bite off the head of anybody who dared to come close to me. I was on the brink of losing everything, and eventually I did.

During this period of my life, my marriage was failing, my friends were disappearing, my nieces found their own careers, and my children grew up and left the nest. The retail business was draining the joy from my life. I needed a change. I decided to sell off and close the stores, one by one. When the last store closed I was exhausted, scared, and for the first time in my life, completely alone.

Totally Out of It

I was out of the country when all this happened.

After I graduated from college, I had the opportunity to move to Santiago, Chile for two years with a volunteer program similar to the Peace Corps. I was doing community organizing, and living with a group of other volunteers in an inner-city neighborhood.

I spent most of my time working with women's groups, and the women of our neighborhood truly opened their homes and their lives to me. They accepted me as an aerobics instructor (even though I had two left feet); taught me to chop an onion (while still holding it in the palm of my hand); and trusted me as a friend (even with my broken Spanish). Together we took classes in tai chi, massage, and other relaxation techniques. Then we brought what we learned back to the neighborhood to pass it on to the other women. I supported them as they taught each other and encouraged them to lean on and share their experiences with each other. In the process I became the student. Isn't that always the way it goes?

While I was away, my mom recorded and sent me

> *cassette tapes with news from home and sound clips from the sitcoms I was missing. She sent me everything... or, almost everything. It was not until years later that I learned about the parts of her life that she left off the tapes. I did not realize just how hard things were for her at this time and how much courage it took for her to start again when she thought she had lost her whole world.*

A Call from the Universe

In times of darkness and loss, if you stay still and listen, answers do come. The fashion fairy tale era may have been over and gone, but another chapter lay ahead. The universe was sending me a huge message: "Move on!"

I had been home alone stewing in my misery for several months when the phone rang. Just in time. It was my fierce retail competitor from my past life. She asked if I would consider putting the rivalry behind us and come work for her as a business consultant. In the midst of this anti-fashion revolution, she wanted a plan to increase revenue by 25%, and she thought I had the energy and the ideas to help get her there.

If I had learned anything running my stores, I knew that the number one rule in sales is "Know Your Customer." So, I created a "Fashion Personality" assessment, which I liked to call the "Myers Briggs of Fashion."[2] Through a series of in-depth questions, I set out to discover the ins and outs of our customers' dressing needs. I sent the survey to hundreds of women throughout the Houston area, then sat back and waited for the results to come in.

I learned that while many of the customers held on to the trusty, relatively conservative, and classic look of "Kate" that got me through the 1980s, there were more women out there. Some customers confirmed that comfort was here to stay and elastic was their lifelong friend. Others longed for styles that were feminine, flirty, and fun. A couple of them wanted bold, creative clothes that made a statement. And don't forget sexy. (Even if they were hesitant to admit it.) Some loved the trends – anything fresh and new.

The survey results gave me an idea. While buying for one customer, Kate, had served me well in the past, following that same branding model was too limiting. Times were changing. There wasn't just one customer out there – there were many. There was an untapped market of great styles centered on the diversity of what our customers wanted: comfort, fun, trends, sex appeal, and creativity.

And then it hit me! I needed to move beyond Kate to create new fashion prototypes, so I set my imagination free. I defined six new women and brought them each to life. Giving each new woman a name and a style, I shared the concept with the staff. Of course, I started with Classic Kate. Then the rest followed: Zenful Zoë, Dramatic Donna, Hanging out Hanna, Trendy Trudy, Girlie Girl Gwen, and Super Sophia.

It became our project. *The Seven Women Project* – I liked the sound of that. I was on to something.

A Hanna Moment

If my mom's first experiences were with "Classic Kate," mine would have been with "Hanging Out Hanna." Her laid-back approach to style sounded like a luxury to me – no dressing up, no putting on make-up to go to a pool party (ask mom about that one too), no muss, no fuss. Just plenty of time to lay around in jeans and let the creative juices flow. I wanted to read, invent stories, and watch lots of "bad TV."

Still, I was intrigued by the so-called project my mom was concocting. If she had created this team of diverse women as a means of discussing their clothes, my own experiences gave me some other ideas. Whether it was the college reporter, the ethnography-loving school graduate student, or the ever-cynical feminist in me, I wanted to know more about these women.

While I thought it was "cute" to think about what each of these women might wear, I was more interested in what lie beneath the surface. What were they like? What made them tick? What inspired them? Did everyone "get" them? What were they reading these days?

I wanted this gang of seven to be stuck in detention like the kids in the 1980s classic movie "The Breakfast Club" and have Principal Vernon assign them 1,000-word essay asking them, "Who you think you are?"

While the fashion was fun, back then it wasn't about the clothes. For me, it was never about the clothes.

I Do a Little Dance on the Cat Walk

As we introduced the customers to Kate, Zoë, Donna, Hanna, Trudy, Gwen, and Sophia, we gave them permission to branch out and explore new possibilities. Our key challenge was to find creative ways to persuade customers to take a risk and try on something their inner Kate might reject, but that Dramatic Donna or Zenful Zoë would embrace.

Our space was large enough to hold in-store events, and so I developed a series of fashion programs designed to help customers learn to "Dress Your Seven Women." The programs were such a success that we soon outgrew the stores. I said good-bye to retail. It was time to take *The Seven Women Project* out into the world.

Through my experiences in the store, I found that one of the best ways to get women to try something new was to get them out of their everyday element and make them part of something completely different. And that is exactly what I did. I put them on the runway.

I encouraged all kinds of women to participate in the fun, claiming that anyone could get up there on stage. Being a model in one of the shows must have been to women what a football fantasy camp is to men. Out under the lights, with the music rocking, everyone had a chance to shine. Even the shyest participants came out of their shells, and the bolder women were more wild and crazy than ever before. I had done runway shows throughout my retail career, but never like this. The events were packed, standing room only. We promised "real women on the runway" and we delivered them in all shapes, sizes, ages, and walks of life. The audiences really got into it as these everyday, girl-next-door-women transformed themselves into runway super-stars.

The "Seven Women on the Runway" event had a little bit of everything - storytelling (maybe a little stand-up), hip music (who could help but do a little runway dance) and high-flying fashion that got the audience clapping and hooting. The magic I had experienced at my first store on the corner was back. The models' clear self-confidence, rock star attitudes, and utter joy were contagious.

That Was Then, This is Now

If the runway was transformative for the models, it was even more so for me. I experienced my own reawakening from the world of retail to a new, expanded calling in the world of coaching, public speaking, and business consulting. All my experiences and life lessons culminated together and I started speaking to audiences around the country on topics

I knew and made my own – branding, leadership, change in the workplace. The seven women were always in my heart – I spoke of them often, and I still do today.

When my mom performed her first "Seven Women on the Runway" show, I had the honor of introducing her. She was so comfortable up on stage and I was such a wreck. But they say that I was beaming when I spoke of how proud I was of her, and I still am. Today, like my mom, I have been through my own kind of transformation. Back from South America for some time now, I have been to graduate school and joined the ranks of public sector technology consultants. Ironically, I struggle with the exact same workplace, branding, and leadership topics that my mom talks about on stage every day.

Because I have always been hungry for community, I became a registered yoga instructor and continue to learn from the men and women that I am supposed to be teaching. I have had heartbreak and bounced back. I have great friends, a home in DC, and a couple of plants that I just barely keep alive. I have an iPod filled with a random assortment of favorites and keep a healthy queue of pop TV shows at the ready.

I still adamantly maintain that it is not about the clothes, but more often than I would like to admit, I have been known to call my mom in a panic to ask her what I should wear.

The Seven Women Project itself has transformed over the years. In the beginning it was all about fashion, dress, and not getting bored with your clothes. But as I continued to speak on the topic, as I listened to the women who came up to me after each show, and as I turned more and more to my daughter to understand her take on the world and these women, the evolution continued.

Today, our intention with *The Seven Women Project* is to take what we have observed over the years and mix it up with what we know now and what we continue to learn. It is a guide to not only *dressing* women, but also celebrating them and all that they have to offer. We are not here to dictate what is right or wrong, but to put a few more options on the table. We invite you to play with us and discover what works for you.

We honor and give gratitude to the amazing women who have come before us – in fiction and in real life – and look forward to meeting many more of you in the days to come.

"Character is how we choose to behave when life doesn't go as planned."[3]

Connie Podesta

"Just do it!"

Nike

"I'll do it!"

Kate

CHAPTER TWO

Classic
Kate

Is There a Little Kate in You?

☐ I admit that I am tougher on myself than I am on others. My personal standards are very high.

☐ My closet is filled with black and white.

☐ I plan what to wear when I am going to an important event or a big day at work.

☐ I juggle multiple tasks and projects at home, with family, and in my community.

☐ I pride myself on getting the job done flawlessly, and as quickly as possible.

☐ I know that even though I work hard and stay late to complete projects, I would do an even better job if I had more time.

☐ I respond quickly to my emails, mobile calls, and text messages, even if I am at the gym or home.

☐ I find that I would rather do things myself than ask others for help, mostly because I want it done right the first time.

☐ I am all for work-life balance. It just means I don't get any sleep.

☐ I am one of the more professional looking women at my workplace.

Who Is Kate?

Kate is the overachiever in each of us.

Kate gets things done. Not just some things, no we're talking everything. That's right. Kate gets everything done, and when Kate is around, everything gets done right.

Kate oozes success. Given the opportunity, Kate doesn't miss a beat. She rolls up her sleeves, takes on responsibility, and tackles the tough problems. Not given the opportunity? Well, then, she just seeks it out for herself. Problem solved.

Kate saves the day, again and again.

It is no wonder that in the 1980s and into the 1990s, Kate was billed as "Superwoman." The big question on everyone's mind back then was, "Can she really do it all?" Career woman. Mom. Community Leader. Significant Other. Friend. You name it. She was it … and, she was great at it all.

Today, Kate is everywhere. True, she can be spotted most easily as a power to behold in the workplace (even if she is sometimes disguised as the mild-mannered "Katie"). But she'll show up at a moment's notice wherever she has a chance to shine. Kate is motivated by her drive to be successful. This success is not only in her career, but also in her family, relationships, and leisure activities.

She is the queen of the "full plate," and always manages to clean it. She has a gold medal in multi-tasking, but always manages to stay on top of the moment. She is fast with a speed dial, powerful in her local motions, able to leap over all obstacles in a single bound. Can she really do it all? You be the judge.

Even so, Kate doesn't need to tell you how great she is (we've got Donna for that). She is polite, gracious, even friendly, but always keeps her ego and her emotions under control. In fact, she prides herself on keeping just about everything under control, and the world is a better place for it.

Kate may not need to toot her own horn, but she does love to be recognized as a person who truly cares about her actions and accomplishments – everything from playing a competitive round of golf to cooking a gourmet meal, from throwing the perfect party to raising smart, well-behaved children. A successful job, money in the bank, a balanced checkbook, and clean sheets on the guest bed are some of the things that may be at the top of Kate's lifelong to-do list. There are many ways that Kate derives her happiness, but all roads lead back to her doing a great job.

No matter where you are in life, Kate is there in your gut keeping you on the straight and narrow, always showing you the "right" way to go. Kate is your conscience, your rule-maker, and gatekeeper. Kate worries about your weight and is concerned if you are not getting enough sleep. Kate is organized, hard working, and self-disciplined. She is that burst of energy that gets you off the couch to organize your pantry.

Kate is the first one to work in morning and she shuts off the lights and closes the office down at night. Kate calls her mother on a regular basis, feeds the kids plenty of fresh vegetables, and takes care of the forgotten hamsters and gold-fish. She drives the neighbor to the doctor, and has time to read a bedtime story to the twins. Kate is a loyal friend, a loving daughter, a hard working employee, a conscientious community leader, a dedicated wife and mother...and a classic, simple dresser.

Some of you might remember the commercial for *"Enjoli"* perfume that was popular in the mid 1970s, and featured a catchy jingle about bringing home the bacon. The perfume claimed to be "the new 8-hour perfume for the 24-hour woman." Sounds like Kate. If you didn't grow up with this commercial, then ask your mom to sing it for you. Chances are she'll remember the commercial lyrics over the original song appropriately titled, "I am Woman." Google *"Enjoli commercial"* to see this classic, retro ad.

Kate Values: High Standards

Our values provide a solid foundation for everything we do and play a huge role in the choices we make in our lives. Values are big for Kate, and she is strong and steadfast in her standards. Although Kate knows that her personal philosophy may continue to evolve from experience and is shaped over time, she is rooted in a set of core values, which she carries throughout each phase in her life.

Some things are classic and timeless. Kate turns to her core beliefs as a trusted guide, successfully navigating her through even the toughest of times.

Kate's Core Values:

Achievement / Success	Grace
Commitment	Security
Control	Family
Dignity	Social Status
Drive	Responsible

"I'm trying to handle everything that's happened to me with a certain amount of grace, dignity and good manners."

Katie Couric

Perception Is Reality

Okay, so no one is really perfect. But admit it, sometimes we think that Kate is. If we look at Kate in the extreme, we may love her or we may hate her. Those of us who want to be like her may idolize her for her perfection, success and the way she pulls herself together like no one else can. On the other hand, too much Kate might make us normal folk jealous, and even a bit catty.

Kate Idealized	Kate Misunderstood
Appropriate	*Always Right*
Classy	*Plastic*
Got it all	*Controlling*
Model family	*Phony*
Perfect	*Perfectionist*
Poised	*Aloof*
Sharp & With-it	*Intimidating*
Successful	*Arrogant*
Superwoman	*Over Achiever*
Under Control	*Bossy*

 "Without discipline, there is no life at all."

Katherine Hepburn

When Do You Need Kate?

The trick is to get your Kate proportions just right. Even if you try to resist her rigid ways, sometimes you need her to give you a kick in the pants or keep driving you to be that successful person that you know you are. Of course, some times are better than others to tap into your inner Kate. Just make sure that you've got Kate along in the following situations.

Be sure to bring Kate:

- To work on Monday, and every day
- When renovating your house and discussing details with the contractors
- To reshape your resume and prepare for your next job interview
- To meet the parents
- When you are drafting your household budget
- When you're writing your New Year's resolutions … and then again in February, when you are just about to scrap those resolutions
- When you've been called into school to talk to your child's teacher
- To your workouts
- When juggling the kids' busy extracurricular schedules
- When you are taking a test, reading a report, or signing on the dotted line
- When organizing a big fund-raising event, hosting your daughter's wedding, or planning a Bar Mitzvah (but don't take her…you have other women for that)

Top 10 *Tips from Kate*

Kate runs a tight ship, whatever kind of ship that may be: at work, at home, and in the community. How does she do it? Well, Kate might tell you that it just comes naturally, but we all know that it takes a remarkable amount of effort to make keeping-on-top-of-things look so easy.

While we know that Kate excels in all life arenas, she is especially exceptional in the workplace, and that is where it starts. According to Kate, if you stay organized and together at work, then all that pulled together-y goodness will naturally stray into the other parts of your life. And voila! Everything falls into place.

So it's easy, right? That's our Kate. Here are Kate's 10 Tips for Keeping Organized and Being Successful on the Job:

1. *Make your first impression count.* First impressions may be based on achievement for men, but whether we like it or not, first impressions are based on appearances for women. Keep yourself well-groomed and smartly dressed, with a strong, well-aligned posture and a warm and genuine smile.

2. *Dress for Success.* Dress to fit into the company culture, and then dress like the leader you aspire to become.

3. *Manage up.* That is, remember that making your boss look good makes you look good. Never surprise your boss. Like you, she doesn't like the unexpected. Stay connected and keep the team in the loop. It will pay off!

4. *Keep your personal to-do list short.* Have no more than six items on your daily list. This goes for your "at home" to-do list too.

5. *Ping yourself.* When an idea hits you and you want to remember it, send yourself a voice message or email from your *BlackBerry, iPhone,* or from your computer.

6. *Take it offline.* Do not start your day by answering emails. Start your day by reviewing, adding, and prioritizing your to-do list.

7. *Think of time in units.* One unit equals five minutes. Then focus on one task, like organizing your desk, and devote one unit of time to it. See how quickly you can accomplish full-scale organization.

8. *Dress sharp on Fridays.* The trick is looking chic in business attire without losing your professionalism. Build your wardrobe with classic pieces and a few accessories. Even though Fridays are casual, you want to look like a leader every day.

9. *Be your own personal MacGyver.* Always keep a roll of dental floss, a bottle of clear nail polish, a travel sewing kit, and a stick of gum in your top drawer at work.

10. *No whining.* Don't waste your time talking about a problem to someone who can do absolutely nothing about it. Solve the problem or bring actionable steps and solutions to someone who can make it happen.

(Okay, let's take it to 11 here… 10 just isn't good enough for an overachiever like our Kate.)

11. *Make friends in high places.* Create and nurture relationships with superiors who have the power to promote you or improve your work situation. This tip works in your personal and professional life.

Dressing *with Kate*
Kate knows the importance of "looking the part."

Kate will be the first to tell you that the first impression is hugely important. We may not like it, but in the first moments of interacting with someone, they are subconsciously sizing us up and making decisions about our abilities based on our appearance. In just a few brief minutes of meeting someone, we tend to let our minds do the heavy lifting, taking in everything from gender, race, ethnicity, and age to approachability, professionalism, confidence, and style. According to the experts, in those first few moments our judging, over-stimulated brains work overtime to take in a slew of other traits and characteristics like: level of education, wealth, trustworthiness, credibility, promptness, honesty, friendliness, courtesy, attractiveness, grooming, job status, attitude, marital status, voice quality, grammar, social status, and even weight. Sigh.

Obviously, some of these things we have control over and some we don't. Kate tends to want to make the most out of everything she has, no matter how she got it. When it comes to the characteristics of dress, she knows she is in control, and it is no wonder that she is always a classic and super-professional dresser. Kate knows that understanding the way you dress is important to the way you are perceived and treated. If you forget this, she warns, you may put yourself at an unnecessary disadvantage from the beginning just because you slacked on the details. And Kate is all about details.

 ## In Kate's Closet

Kate's taste is rooted in appropriateness, not necessarily trends. She focuses on clothes, accessories, and other products that combine great personal style with long-lasting utility. The fundamental principles of Kate's philosophy of style dictate clean, modern shapes with a nod to the classics, an element of surprise, and then another nod to the classics.

When you take a peek into Kate's closet, you know she is super-successful. With a little help from the Elfa closet gurus from the Container Store, it is clear that Kate has assembled a wardrobe solution with the right pieces to give her that stylish, yet professional, "getting down to business" look that exudes confidence and attracts success.

Here are some key pieces that you will find in Kate's closet:

- *Three-piece classic black suit with a fitted jacket, slim skirt, and trousers*
- *Several pair of good quality slacks in black, brown, gray, and beige*
- *Black pencil skirt*
- *High quality khakis and dark jeans*
- *Crisp white blouse*
- *Knit tanks and tees in black, white, and beige*
- *Black and off-white Cashmere cardigan*
- *High quality leather purse*

- *Classic, "expensive-looking" gold and silver link watch*
- *Fitted trench coat or jacket*
- *Black sheath dress that can be dressed up or down*
- *Silver and gold hoops*
- *Several pair of current, in-style shoes and boots*
- *Workout clothes and classy lingerie*

More Tips from Kate

Kate just can't stop telling us what to do, can she? But if you haven't figured it out yet, Kate knows her stuff. Sure, you could study her style and copy her closet, but why not take a few more lessons from the Queen of Classics. Here are a few wardrobe tips from Kate that might help you grow your basics and create your own career style as you commit to dressing with intention.

Organize your closet for speed dressing and good decision making. Organize your closet in such a way that you have your daily work clothes ready and accessible. Do you have the right slacks for your workplace and appropriate tops that keep you looking pulled together every day? Now is the time to make a list of what's missing and replace some of your worn pieces with items you need to look like someone who should be taken seriously. Keep it simple. Arrange your work clothes together in one spot in your closet. Organinize your items by category for easy access. You do not need to reinvent the wheel every morning.

Identify your top "knock-'em-dead" outfit. Have one great outfit for when you need to pull out all the stops. For some women, it could be a classic yet contemporary suit by Theory suit or a fabulous blouse by Eye. Whatever you choose, make sure it not only looks and feels good, but also makes you feel good about yourself when you wear it. This is the outfit that you can count on for the confidence boost to get you through any professional situation.

> *Develop a great relationship with a seamstress or a tailor.* Have your clothes altered professionally. Take a tip from the most successful CEOs and always get your clothes tailored to fit your body perfectly, even your jeans. Find a reliable cleaner while you are at it. Keep your great pieces looking as great as you.

Some of Kate's Favorite Designers and Labels

Kate is smart and savvy enough to know that dressing well does not necessarily mean you have to go to a top designer and buy the most expensive articles of clothing. Still, there are some designers and labels that Kate loves to splurge on, including:

Ann Taylor	*Eye*
Armani	*Faconnable*
Banana Republic (great suits!)	*Ellen Tracey*
Coach	*St. John*
Donna Degnan	*Tahari*
Donna Karen (knits)	*Three Dot Tees*
Theory	*Finley Blouses*
J'Envie	*Jones of New York*
Lafayette 148	*Max Mara*
Michael Kors	*Hermes*
Kate Spade	

Famous Kates

Do you recognize a little Kate in any of these famous women?

Anna Wintour   Maria Bartiromo
Audrey Hepburn   Princess Grace
Diane Sawyer   Nicole Kidman
Cathie Black   Vanessa Williams
Hillary Clinton   Katie Couric
Katharine Hepburn Halle Berry
Charlotte York   Gwen Ifill
Ann Curry   Chandra Wilson
Suze Orman   Martha Stewart

 ## Kate's Bookshelf

A few of the books on Kate's nightstand include:

- *Women & Money: Owning the Power to Control Your Destiny*, by Suze Orman
- *Basic Black*, by Cathie Black
- *Time Management From the Inside Out*, by Julie Morgenstern
- *Mothers on the Fast Track: How a New Generation Can Balance Family and Careers*, by Mary Ann & Mason Eve Mason Ekman
- *Nice Girls Don't Get the Corner Office: 101 Unconscious Mistakes Women Make That Sabotage Their Careers*, by Lois P. Frankel
- *The Third Shift: Managing Hard Choices in Our Careers, Homes and Lives as Women*, by Michele Bolton

- *Entertaining*, by Martha Stewart
- *Smart Women Finish Rich: Nine Steps to Achieving Financial Security and Funding Your Dreams*, by Dave Bach

And how about a fiction book just for kicks: *I Don't Know How She Does It* by Allison Pearson...even the main character's name is Kate! We swear we were writing this long before the book came out, but Kate Reddy is soooo Kate.

 ## Movies on Kate's Netflix Queue

Kate doesn't really have time to watch TV, but she does enjoy the efficiency of Netflix arriving at her door. If she did have time to watch anything, maybe these would come down off her queue into her home theater:

Absence of Malice	*The September Issue*
Mr. Mom	*Baby Boom*
The Way We Were	*Up in the Air*
Breakfast at Tiffany's	*Woman of the Year*
Broadcast News	*Million Dollar Baby*
Devil Wears Prada	*Baby Mama*
His Girl Friday	*One Fine Day*
The Incredibles	
Working Girl	
Aliens	
Network	
Nine to Five	
Sense and Sensibility	

Superhero *or Fairy Tale?*

Once upon a time there was a beautiful, successful and very got-it-together young woman named Kate. Kate had done everything right – she was the first in her family to go to college, graduated with honors, got a job, and then got her graduate degree going to night school. Kate married well and had two great kids.

Kate was exceptionally good at her job, but she was just as good at keeping her whole life in tiptop shape when she left the office. Kate was a natural born juggler – throw her a plate, and she'd wipe it clean and keep it circling in the air along with that tennis ball, bowling pin, blow torch, or whatever else she had juggling up there. There have been countless tales told about Kate's throwing and catching of work, kids, extended family, and community activities without a fumble.

How did Kate do it all? How she balanced her family life, her job, and her me-time remains a mystery. Legend has it, if she couldn't sneak away from work at lunch then she did her workout at 5 a.m. while everyone else was asleep. This was like "magic time" because it didn't cut into anyone else's schedule – she could still get the kids ready for day care and get her self to the office on time. The only trick was staying awake during meetings, and she just might have had that one down too.

This is the story that we have been told – this legend of Kate. In the 1980s, we were told that women could do it all. In the 1990s, we were *still* told that we could do it all, but that we should have planned better when to have children. Today, we just throw up our hands as we're told we are unhappy. Secretly, under the dark of night, the legend of perfect Kate is still passed down in one form or another from one generation to the next.

In reality, not all of these stories have the happily-ever-after ending. Don't get us wrong, some do – handsome prince and all – but some end with Kate feeling tired, burnt out, and searching the Internet, a little on the empty side.

That's where the rest of the seven women come in – riding to the rescue on white horses, armed with smelling salts, and brandishing kisses of true love. Bringing gifts of inner awareness (Zoë), self-confidence (Donna), personal time-outs (Hanna), curiosity (Trudy), femininity (Gwen), and wisdom (Sophia). All of these women are inside each of us, ready to save the day one experience at a time. And, sure, this could turn out to be its own kind of fairy tale – or maybe a *Choose Your Own Adventure* story – but whatever you call it, it is quite a ride.

"Whatever you are waiting for – peace of mind, contentment, grace, the inner awareness of Simple Abundance--it will surely come, but only when you are ready to receive it with an open and grateful heart." [4]

Sarah Ban Breathnach

CHAPTER THREE

Zenful
Zoë

Is There a Little Zoë in You?

☐ Deep down I know that we are all connected to each other in some way.

☐ I enjoy my quiet "alone time" and use that opportunity to practice being more mindful and centered.

☐ I know the power of positive thinking. I believe that if you can change your thinking, you can change your life.

☐ I think about how something feels against my body before I put it on. I love textures and prefer natural fibers.

☐ I listen to my inner voice and make decisions for my life after searching within myself.

☐ I practice yoga, meditation, or some kind of spiritual exercise.

☐ At the end of a busy day, there is nothing more rewarding than a nice hot bath. Often I add to the experience by lighting a few candles and playing soothing music.

☐ I have an assortment of shawls, scarves, and pashminas. I like the feeling of being wrapped in comfort.

☐ I am curious about different religions, philosophies, customs, and beliefs.

☐ I have created a vision board and practice bringing intention and a sense of purpose to my daily life.

Who Is Zoë

Zoë is the inner spirit, self-nurturer, and guiding voice in each of us.

Kate has worked hard to create and maintain the image that everything in her life is A-okay. And to those of us on the outside, we believe that it is. But what happens when – for whatever reason – Kate just can't do it any more? What happens when the over-scheduled life spirals out of control? When the unexpected comes crashing in out of nowhere? What happens when Kate's version of "perfect" just isn't good enough?

Zoë happens.

Zoë has been trying to flag us down and get our attention for a long time. She has tried to calm our anxious minds and win over our quickly beating hearts. She has tried to get us to stop and smell the flowers. She has tried to get us to take a well-deserved, long-overdue rest. But we have been too busy being busy to listen.

But little by little, it seems that the tides are finally turning towards Zoë and she is beginning to get through to us. All the whisperings of the sweet nothings of relaxation has finally begun to pay off, and we are beginning to allow ourselves to be still and listen. Maybe it is because we are all just getting tired. Maybe this rapid-fire life is wearing us down. Or maybe, just maybe, we are starting to realize there is more to it all. Instead of pushing Zoë to the back of our minds, we are able to consider the possibility that there is something out there that is bigger than all of this.

If Kate is about taking action, Zoë is about finding the purpose or intention in that action. Kate is the doing and Zoë is the being. Zoë is not afraid to ask the big question, "What are we here for?"

As today's world becomes more focused on getting things done and getting ahead, Zoë is becoming less of a foreign concept and more visible to the everyday world. Perhaps it is because she is needed now more than ever. Perhaps it is because of the recent outpouring of books and videos that have everyone talking, such as *The Secret* and the *Power of Now*. Perhaps it is simply because Zoë has Oprah as her number one promoter.

For whatever reason, Zoë is starting to be seen as less "out-there" and becoming more mainstream. As scented candles, yoga studios, and 10-minute meditations become increasingly prevalent, we are beginning to hear more Zoë stories. Yoga instructor, massage therapist, body worker, preacher, healer, spiritual guide, teacher, and friend. Zoë's roles are many. But however she manifests it, at her essence, Zoë is our spirit, our soul, and our inner peace.

She is our caretaker and our touchstone. Not only does she have the capacity to love and nurture her children, parents, partner, and friends, but Zoë also has abundance of love to nurture herself. Zoë is soothing. Her healing restores us. She quiets us down after the challenges of the day. She draws our bath, puts on soothing music, and covers our bodies in creams and lotions. Zoë knows that we must take care of ourselves, protect ourselves, and love ourselves before we can be effective in giving to others.

Some call her our direct line to the divine, others say she is our inner voice. However you envision her, Zoë is inside each of us to guide us through this life. She is our north star, our personal compass, and the sensibility that knows us deep within. She knows that it's in the peaceful, quiet times we are truly able to connect with our inner self.

But let's keep it simple. Zenful Zoë is about the Ahhhhhh. She remembers to breathe. She is about the healing powers of relaxation, meditation and letting all the stress of our world wash away as we evolve, grow, and discover our purpose.

 ## Zoë Values: Universal Connection

Core beliefs and values are especially important to Zoë since these universal values are what drive her and give her life and actions meaning. Zoë is about spirituality in action. No matter what religion a person practices, Zoë believes there are universal values, which we embrace in our journey to be happier, more loving people.

Zoë's Core Values:

Balance	*Love of self and others*
Being grounded and centered	*Inspiration*
Connection	*Mindfulness*
Loving kindness	*Nurturing and healing*
Purpose	*Spirit*
Service	*Abundance*

Perception Is Reality

Zoë teaches us that it's not "all or nothing" when it comes to bringing a little zenful zip to our lives. The trick is not necessarily learning to take ourselves out of the world we live in, but learning how to truly be in this world: aware, connected, and alive. Too much Zoë and we might be living in the clouds; too little and we might be one panic attack away from a breakdown.

Zoë wants you to be your own spiritual guide – whatever that means to you – and wants you to be at home in your own style and preferences. You can be your own form of connectedness and your own sense of spirituality. You don't have to quit your day job and move to an ashram in the mountains to find inner peace. Unless of course you want to. The challenge is getting the porridge just right, enjoying the ahhhh, and bringing ourselves that much closer to our hearts' desires.

Zoë Idealized	Zoë Misunderstood
Always calm, in the moment	*Granola*
In touch with the Divine	*Holier-than-thou*
Harmonious	*New Age-y*
In tune with body and mind	*Not in the real world*

Never gets stressed out	*Naive*
Open heart	*Push over*
Practices what she preaches	*Judgmental*
Radiates inner beauty	*Trivial*
Sees how we're all connected	*Sings Kumba Ya*
Meets her spiritual needs	*Dreamer*

When Do You Need Zoë?

Without even having to go anywhere near the "there-must-be-something-bigger-out-there" spiritual side, one of the key motivators for tapping into Zoë may have to do with the other "S" word – stress. No need to sugarcoat it. No use denying it. Americans are totally stressed out.

Is there any wonder why? Between rising unemployment, unbelievable national debt, and the current economic downturn, many of us are at our financial wits' end. And if worrying about our financial future doesn't keep us up at night, we can take our pick from any combination of work-related stress factors, family-related triggers, health concerns, political issues, and social worries. There's no doubt that these are challenging times: in our homes, across the country, and throughout the world. It is hard enough to keep from getting stressed out reading the paper (if it hasn't already gone under), or even this paragraph.

If we manage to keep our cool inspite of it all, even if we don't consider ourselves among the continually stressed, the over-stressed, or the Calgon-Take-Me-Away stressed, there are moments when we could all use a little Zoë in our lives.

Don't forget to keep Zoë close at these times:

- At the end of the day when it is time to unwind
- When you have to make a life decision and you need to get out of your head and into yourself
- When you are frustrated with friends, children or spouse, or have had it with your job, boss, or teammates
- When your plane is delayed, the train breaks down, or you are stuck in traffic and just about ready to lash out at a fellow traveler or driver
- When your college graduate comes home to live for a year ... or so
- When you are feeling fatigue, having trouble sleeping, or just got high-cholesterol results back from the doctor
- When you are caring for an aging family member
- When you are a new mom
- When you are laid off or looking for a new job
- When it's Friday at 4:30 p.m. and everyone's going home. You, on the other hand, still have incomplete projects on your desk and at least four hours of work ahead of you before you can leave
- When you have been out all day and you open the door to a house full of kids, your husband watching TV, an empty ice cream container out on the counter, dirty dishes in the sink, chips and crackers spilled across the coffee table, half-filled Coke glasses everywhere, ice melting on the floor, newspapers all across the sofa, wet towels in the hall, and the dog hasn't been out since you left. Zoë come to me now! Breathe....

Top 10 Tips *from Zoë*
For getting into the relaxation groove and staying there

Starting to recognize the outcomes of the stressful world we live in might be the first step to addressing the symptoms of stress, but Zoë takes a broader view. Zoë embraces a holistic, integrated approach to health and overall living in which reducing stress is just one of the positive results that come from opening herself up to the endless possibilities that life offers and connecting to a greater energy. Zoë doesn't just want this for herself. She wants to see you healthy, energized, and living your best life.

Of course, the best thing about all this Zoë stuff is that deep down we know it already. It is intuitive, sometimes we just forget. Her tips are simple, yet big in impact. Here are a couple helpful reminders from Zoë:

1. *Take bite-sized pieces.* When it comes to relaxation techniques, start small and build up. Start with just 10 minutes of something, whether it is mediation, yoga, breathing, or just getting out of the house and going on a walk. Test it out. See how it works for you. Then, build up and consider adding more when the time is right. 10 minutes just doesn't seem long enough? Research says it is. According to the *Yoga Journal*, even 10 minutes of meditation each day is enough to make a difference in reducing stress and boosting the immune system. However you choose to do it, Zoë urges you to make relaxation an integrated part of your daily, weekly, or monthly routine.

2. *Keep moving.* Just because you are trying to be more relaxed doesn't mean you have to give over to your inner slacker (unless, of course, you're Hanna). Get the blood pumping, do some yoga movements (asana), or get a little exercise. Again, find something you like to do. Keep it simple but remember, it is recommended that we all get at least 30 minutes of exercise a day to keep the mind and body healthy. The Kate in you might want to push herself just a little more – train for a long run, take up rock climbing (meditation on rock, yum), or join a movement class that meets weekly or even daily. Whatever gets you out there, make it a regular part of your life. But don't let it stress you out. Exercise should be fun and inspiring.

3. *Get some sleep.* While it may be stating the obvious: sleep is good; sleep deprivation is bad. While you sleep, your brain goes through a memory store and memory consolidation, where it sorts out what to keep and what to discard. Studies show that with enough sleep you will remember things better, improve complex problem-solving, and be a generally more productive person. For something new, "Yoga Nidra" is a form of guided relaxation that helps you get in touch with your inner intentions while at the same time getting some much needed rest. They say that one hour of Yoga Nidra is like four hours of regular sleep. Can you beat it? It's like a sleep sale!

4. *Rock your chakras.* You might be a fan of chanting, drum circles, or good old fashion rock and roll, but whatever you prefer, don't be afraid to get your groove on. Let the music move you. You might be surprised how music can lift your spirit, rejuvenate your energy stores, and get the blood flowing. We once knew a Zoë who liked to start her yogic dance party with the Beastie Boys' instrumental album followed by the modernly mystic hip hop tunes of M.C. Yogi. Some of Zoë's more chantalicious favorite performers include Krishna Das, Wah!, David Stringer, and Yogini chantress Amy Ippoliti's *Invocation*. Take a chance. You never know where you'll find the gems.

5. *Eat something, will you?* You know the drill – your body is a temple, so treat it like one. Again, the rules are many (sometimes even contradictory), so figure out what works for you and your belief system. Need a couple of good rules to get you started? Reduce caffeine or cut it out all together. Avoid refined sugar, white flour, and red meat. Listen to Oprah and don't eat after 10 p.m. (Not a grape!)

6. *Just breathe.* Practice deep breathing. In the yogic tradition, the study of pranyama is the practice of breathing. It is not about controlling the life force, or breath, but learning to flow with it. Zoë says we should all take some time to learn about the breath – not just all that upper chest breathing that we do when we are scared or anxious, but really deep breathing from the diaphragm, which allows us to tap into other parts of ourselves. Although we do it every day, really learning to breathe can be a breath of fresh air (so to speak). There are all kinds of breathing techniques – varying in level of complexity – that can help restore calm and strengthen us from the inside out.

7. *Thank your lucky stars.* "Gratitude is the most passionate transformative force in the cosmos," promises

Sarah Ban Breathnach, author of *Simple Abundance*. Gratitude journaling is a way to count your blessings in a simple day-by-day journal. Ban Breathnach says "if you give thanks for five gifts every day, in two months you may not look at your life in the same way as you might now." [5] After 60 days of journaling you will be more aware of the gifts that life bestows on you and focus less on what's wrong in your life. Better yet, pass it on. Find a couple of trusted friends who want to play along and email each other your daily gratitude lists. It is a great way to build community and inspire each other.

8. *Feel free to sneak it in.* You might be surprised that you are able to find a little bit of time each day for quiet and solitude, even if you have to trick yourself into it. For some of us, it could be driving home from work with the radio off, silencing our phone or Black-Berry during the evening meal, or finding online tools to remind us to practice our ten-minute meditations. Or, it could be finding "consciousness" while doing something ordinary like washing the dishes. One of Zoë's big time heroes, Thich Nhat Hanh, a Buddist monk, encourages us to focus on being in the present and to practice mindfulness while performing even the simplest of tasks.

9. *Stay connected.* When you think about people you care about, pick up the phone and call them. Staying connected to a community can go a long way in reducing stress. A landmark UCLA study reveals that friendships between women are vitally important and necessary for a woman's well being. The study suggests that female friendships soothe our stress, fill any emo-

tional gaps in our marriage, and connect us to our authentic self. Scientists now suspect that spending time with our friends can actually counteract sadness and the stress that many of us experience on a daily basis.

10. *Don't let relaxing stress you out.* When finding time to de-stress … Enjoy! This is not a chore. Have fun with it. It's okay to feel good. LAUGH! Daily laughter can be a cure. Laughter empowers your immune system.

Dressing *with Zoë*
Zoë knows it's all about what's on the inside, but likes to feel good in what she wears on the outside

There is something about Zoë that may feel a bit lofty, kooky, or even unattainable. For some of us, tapping into Zoë's zenful side may be as easy as slipping on a comfortable pair of Birkenstocks and simply aligning ourselves with the whole universe (no problem!). But for the rest of us, not so much. It takes a little bit of effort, and a whole lot of being in the right frame of mind. For Zoë, sometimes a change of clothes is the first step to helping her get her attitude and intention moving in the right direction.

Just like with costume changes in the movies or on stage, a change of clothes can help us delineate the different phases of the day. At the end of a long day at the office or when you're with the kids, change your clothes – shed your work clothes and get into your "life" clothes – whether that means getting ready for exercise, cooking, or relaxing. Let your own wardrobe changes be a sign to you that it is time to slow down or energize up, and go with it.

Inside Zoë's Closet

Peering into Zoë's closet you may come face to face with Mother Nature personified. Zoë has piles of earthy, natural clothes that express to the outside world the way that Zoë feels on the inside. Her clothes, accessories, and other closet trinkets reflect her style. Here's what you'll find:

Natural fibers
Lots of elastic
Tank tops and tees
Tunic or baby-doll tops
Cream, beige, off-white, sand, earth, and olive tones
Ethnic prints and jewelry
Hand knit scarves and luxurious pashminas
Broom skirts
Yoga or exercise pants
Woven tote
Sandals / Clogs
Mala beads and crystal jewelry
Pieces she picked up from flea markets and art festivals
Reusable grocery bags

Some of Zoë's Favorite Designers and Labels

Zoë may not get excited about labels and designers, but that doesn't mean she doesn't like to shop. She has been spotted looking for natural necessities at the likes of Whole Foods and Aveda, flea markets, yoga stores, and even art festivals. So much of what she likes she can even get online, but Zoë prefers touching her goods and loves supporting local vendors and friends. Although you don't typically have to search far to find Zoë-inspired clothes, there are some lines and labels that go a long way to capture her essence, including:

Eileen Fisher
James Perse
Peace Love Mom
Danskin
Lululemon
Stonewear Designs
Beckons

Hyde
Salaam
Be Present
Inner Waves Maui
Prana
TranquiliT
CrocusPocus Designs

 ## Famous Zoës

Do you recognize Zoë in any of these famous people?

Ashley Judd
Caroline Myss
Cheryl Richardson
Christy Turlington
Debbie Ford
Suzanne Somers
Gwyneth Paltrow
India Arie

Iyanlla Vanzant
Naomi Watts
Alicia Silverstone
Mandy Ingber
Olivia Newton John
Seane Corn
Zooey Deschanel
Trudie Styler

 ## Zoë's Bookshelf

Zoë loves to learn about herself, her body and the world around her. It is no surprise then that Zoë's bookshelf is teeming with a wide range of books, magazines, and other audio/visual media. Below is a sampling of Zoë's latest reads and reference materials, including recommended reading to accompany her list of tips. In addition to the items listed below,

Zoë also stays up to date on the latest health research, articles, and the growing selection of web offerings for holistic living.

General Interest

- *The Artist's Way: A Spiritual Path to Higher Creativity*, by Julia Cameron
- *Finding Your Own North Star: Claiming the Life You Were Meant to Live*, by Martha Beck
- *The Four Agreements*, by Don Miguel Ruiz
- *Go Green Live Rich*, by David Bach & Hillary Rosner
- *The Power of Now* and *A New Earth*, by Eckhart Tolle
- *The Power of Intention*, by Wayne Dyer
- *Sacred Contracts* and *Anatomy of the Spirit: The Seven Stages of Power and Healing*, by Caroline Myss
- *The Secret*, by Rhonda Byrne
- *The Spontaneous Fulfillment of Desire*, by Deepak Chopra

Meditation, Breathing and Yoga

- *Eastern Body Western Mind: Psychology and the Chakra System as a Path to Self*, by Anodea Judith
- *The Heart of Meditation: Pathways to Deeper Experiences*, by Sally Kempton (Swami Durganda). Out of print; a gem if you can find it.
- *Light on Yoga*, by BKS Iyengar
- *The Miracle of Mindfulness*, by Thich Nhat Hanh
- *Relax and Renew: Restful Yoga For Stressful Times*, by Judith Lasater
- *Yoga Nidra, the Meditative Heart of Yoga*, by Richard Miller
- Magazines like: *Ascent, Fit Yoga, Utne Reader, Spirituality and Health*, and *Yoga Journal*.

Movies on Zoe's Netflix Queue

A Beautiful Mind
Dead Poet's Society
The Lion King
Avatar
Gandhi
I ♥ Huckabees
An Inconvenient Truth
The Secret
Sliding Doors
What the Bleep Do We Know?
Eternal Sunshine of the Spotless Mind

Gorrillas in the Mist
Planet Earth 2000
Practical Magic
Momento
Lord of the Rings Trilogy
Silkwood
Whale Rider
March of the Penguins
The Cove

Zoë also depends on Yoga instructional cds and videos. One of our favorite DVDs is Desirèe Rumbaugh's *Yoga to the Rescue: Feel Good from Head to Toe*, but there are tons of great cds and videos at Amazon, various yoga sites online, or in your local yoga studio. Just ask your yogini friends for the instructors they are drawn to and check them out.

"We do this practice to learn how to align our bodies and our minds with our Devine Nature which is pure positive bliss."

Desirée Rumbaugh

Vision 101: *Set Your Intention*

If Kate is all about setting goals and objectives for living a successful life, Zoë wants to know what's your intention? What is your big picture ideal? Your wildest dream? Your vision for a better tomorrow?

Zoë lets her imagination run wild, and she invites the universe to play along at home. Zoë believes that if she allows herself to create and cultivate a vision of the life that she wants to live, then the universe will conspire to make things happen. But this is not about willy-nilly fleeting interests. No, Zoë isn't at all flippant-like; she has given this some serious thought. She really wants it, and she calls it by name. Zoë is about being steadfast, clear, and focused in her greater life path. Action follows intent.

Creating a vision board is one of Zoë's favorite do-it-yourself projects. It is a great tool that helps her get clarity around what it is that she really wants in her life. Building a vision board helps whoever is behind the visioning wheel clearly identify and describe her dreams and desires, and gives her the ability to manifest what she wants in her life. By naming the vision and releasing it out into the universe, the idea is that the power of the vision will attract into her life these desires, making her dream a reality.

Creating your vision board is energizing, creative, fun, and easy. So get out the scissors and glue stick. It's creatin' time.

Five Easy Steps to a More Visioning You

Here's what you need:

- *A collection of magazines, catalogs, photos, images from the web*
- *A photo of YOU*
- *One large poster board*
- *Scissors (round tips please)*
- *Glue stick, rubber cement, or tape*
- *Variety of markers, crayons, or finger paint*

Step 1. Set 45 to 60 minutes aside! Put on some soothing music, close your eyes, and set your intention. Take some deep breaths and let go, clear your mind of the clutter, and focus on you and what you want. Let the images come into your mind and stay with them for a moment.

Step 2. Begin by flipping through the magazines and start tearing out images and words that resonate with you. Have fun with it. Make a big pile of images and phrases and words.

Step 3. Go through the images and begin to lay your absolute favorites on the board. Eliminate any images that you do not absolutely love. Here is where your intention comes into play. What is it that you really want?

Step 4. Glue yourself in the center – focus on what YOU want and then glue everything onto the board that reflects your desires. Add writing if you want.

Step 5. Hang your vision board in a place where you will see it often. Make it happen.

Karen McCullough's vision board

"Drama is very important in life: You have to come on with a bang. You never want to go out with a whimper."

Julia Child

CHAPTER FOUR

Dramatic
Donna

Is There a Little Donna in You?

☐ I love color, bold prints, striking black, and unique jewelry.

☐ If I am in a group of introverts I feel responsible to keep the conversation alive and bubbling.

☐ If I like you and respect you I will promote you.

☐ I understand the importance of being able to voice my accomplishments and my opinions.

☐ People remember me – what I say, what I do, and what I wear. I definitely stand out in a crowd.

☐ Networking is a natural activity for me. I do not stress out when attending events where I know no one. I will soon be talking and connecting.

☐ I have conquered the "fear of asking' and I am comfortable speaking up for what I want.

☐ I have been called a "go getter" and I love it!

☐ I am aware of my talents and I have never been accused of lacking self-confidence.

☐ It's a good thing I showed up. This dinner party would have been a flop.

Who is Donna ?

Donna is the confident, powerful voice in each of us.

As a child, Donna was the girl who sat in the front row with her hand constantly up in the air waving with enthusiasm.

"Oh! Me! Me! Call on meeee!" she would shout.

It wasn't that she was a teacher's pet. She may not have even particularly liked that subject, but she knew what she knew and she made a point to tell everyone. She wasn't afraid to speak her mind, to give her opinion, and to say it out loud.

As Donna grew up, her self-awareness grew with her. She became confident and powerful, and by the time she was a young adult, she had unleashed what she saw as her true self. She squashed any fear that crossed her path and stuck steadfastly to cultivating her vision of herself. She became a leader and a personal marketing maverick. She learned early that sometimes you just have to get over yourself, get your fear behind you, and push yourself to do whatever it's going to take to get you where you need to be.

Donna is the external self-assurance that we are magnetically attracted to. She is the Diva of Confidence. Donna is our Number One Fan, our personal cheerleader, our private PR firm, and our confident and powerful voice. She is the positive vision that we have of ourselves. Donna rocks and she makes each of us into our very own rock star.

Donna is the one who knows the real you, and loves what she sees! She sees you as successful and effective. She knows all of your accomplishments and remembers every one of them. In the game of life, Donna is our personal scorecard and posts all the successes and triumphs we have had, no matter how big or insignificant they may have seemed to us at the time.

Donna laughs through our pain. She sees our greatness, even if it frightens us. She is fearless, powerful, assertive, and the risk-taker that we dream of being. Donna has the courage and confidence to say yes to life, and to overcome the imposter syndrome, that voice in our head that tells us we have fooled everyone and that we are not as good as we think we are.

Donna says, "You *are* as good as they think you are, in fact, you are better."

Donna knows that it takes using all that we have inside of us to get the true joys and successes that life has to offer, and she is there to help guide us along the way.

For too long, research was suggesting that there weren't many Donnas in our elementary schools. Girls were taught to be quiet, they were rewarded for being good, and they tended to keep their ideas to themselves. With awareness and the "girl power" movement, this trend has been changing, and there is a whole new generation of Donnas out there – bounding up to us, speaking their minds, and getting their hands up waving.

 ## Donna's Values: Her Impeccable Brand

Donna knows the importance of personal branding and she asks you, "What are you known for?" Your personal brand is what others think of when your name is mentioned.

A few years back, the only people who thought about "personal branding" were politicians, actors, and, of course, Donna. They all understood that creating an identifiable brand was not just for inanimate products anymore. Move over Coke and Disney, branding took years off Oprah's "getting noticed curve." Is it any wonder Prince could actually get away with becoming a symbol? His brand as an eccentric musical genius was that strong.

Ask Donna what her assets are and she will rattle them off. She is comfortable with her talents and knows how and when to use them, creating a memorable brand for herself. She is a firm believer that your brand potential is so powerful that it may determine your success and even your future.

Donna's Core Values:

Assertiveness	*Initiative*
Courage	*Optimism*
Determination	*Recognition*
Fame	*Risk-taking*
Fearlessness	*Distinctiveness*

Perception Is Reality

Donna says and does the outrageously bold things that we might never have the courage to do…without a stiff drink or two. She is fearless and can hold court at even the most boring dinner parties. And if we are being totally honest, in big doses, Donna may be hard for some of us to swallow. Sure, we all want to be confident and self-assured. But at what point does that cross the line into being an annoying braggart, self-centered, and downright obnoxious?

If your friends are rolling their eyes or embarrassed to be seen with your big, crazy Donna self, it may be that your Donna is just a teensy bit too big for her britches. Or more likely, as Donna would say, you just need new friends.

Donna Idealized	Donna Misunderstood
Risk-taker	*Opportunist*
Self-promoter	*Self-absorbed*
Bold	*Loud*
Extroverted	*Embarrassing*
Conversationalist	*Dominator*
Powerful	*Overbearing*
Interactive	*Exhibitionist*
Fun Loving	*Wild*
Lives on the Edge	*Unstable*
Assertive	*Aggressive*

When Do You Need Donna?

Finding a balanced Donna is a challenge in itself. But you're a rock star, remember? Suck it up. Face the task because you need her, especially in the following situations:

- At work when you want to be noticed for the good that you do, not in a Michael Scott of *The Office* way, or because you can Xerox your butt at the company party (do people really do that anymore?)
- When you are ready to be seen and stop being invisible
- When writing your elevator speech. Be able to tell your "story" in 30 seconds or less
- At any networking event
- When writing a memorable cover letter or updating your resume
- The day you get laid off, or you decide to quit your job and go out on your own
- Any time you do something remarkable and are ready to share it with the world
- At your job interview, performance review or giving a presentation (okay, dress like Kate, but come armed with the Donna-tude)
- When you are attending a conference or event where you know hardly anyone
- For a night on the town, anything outrageous will do

"If you don't like what you see, reinvent yourself." [6]

Christine Comoford-Lynch

Top 10 *Tips from Donna*
How to get and stay noticed!

1. *Capitalize on your distinctiveness.* What are you an expert in? Get clear on your expertise and then practice believing it. You have to believe in yourself before we can believe in you. Have the courage to stand apart from the crowd, and then be able to articulate what it is that you do really well. It's time to get energized, excited, and enthusiastic about who you are, what you do, and how you do it!

2. *Grow a thick skin.* If you are really interested in discovering your personal brand, find out what others think of you. Take the following questions to your clients, supervisors, and colleagues – anyone whose opinion you truly respect. Ask them to give you a one-word response to each question, and then compare their answers to how YOU see yourself. You may find you need a brand adjustment.

- What do you see as my dominant personality trait?
- What value or principle do you most closely associate with me?
- What skill, ability, or talent comes to mind when you think of me?
- How do you describe me to others who have never met me?

3. *Show up!* Get out from behind the TV and stop watching those reality shows (unless you're the one on the tube). You have to be out there getting attention and getting noticed. Create the buzz about you. The last thing you need to hear is, "Donna who?"

4. *Talk to strangers.* You never know who is sitting next to you on the plane or standing behind you in the movie line. Networking isn't a dirty word. Practice small talk and know how to strike up a conversation. As for strangers at work, don't assume that most people in your organization know you. Introduce yourself, even to a person you've already met once or twice. Chances are they will be grateful to hear your name again. (Think Denny Crane on *Boston Legal*. He's the man who walks around introducing himself to anyone who will listen; he just assumes he is as famous as a rock star, until pretty soon, he is.)

5. *Build your success on referrals and testimonials.* If someone has something great to say about you, make it official. Get the compliments in writing. You'll be glad you did.

6. *Give back by volunteering your time and talents.* Stay active in your community and take the time to contribute to the folks that sustain you.

7. *Register your name.com and then start writing newsletters, or better yet, start blogging.* Electronic social networking is not just for Trudy.

8. *Ask or you'll never receive.* Get yourself assigned to a high-profile project or one that puts you in contact with someone in power who will see your skill and talents first hand. The people forming opinions about you rarely see your day-to-day, on-the-job greatness. If you aren't able to work directly with them, they will rely on you to keep them in the loop – learn to tell them about your experiences with a positive, energetic and non-obnoxious style. Practice, practice, practice.

9. *Partner with a "Brag-buddy" to toot your own horn and create a buzz about your work.* Each of you will brag about the other person whenever possible. In her book *Brag!*, Peggy Klause writes about two U.S. Naval Academy graduates made a pact to brag like crazy about each other. They became the two youngest admirals ever, tooting their way through naval history. [7]

10. *Get into ACTION!* Your actions speak volumes about who you are and your brand. Michael Eisner once said that your personal brand is a living entity – it is enriched or undermined cumulatively over time. Your brand is the product of a thousand small gestures, so what are you doing? What steps are you taking to create a more passionate and relevant you? When you wake up tomorrow do something different than you usually do each morning. Make a real change in your behavior, and make it stick

Dressing *with Donna*
Donna knows how to make sure she is in the spotlight.

Donna loves attention and her style is as fearless as she is. She is bodacious, outrageous, and exciting. Her clothing combinations are bold and cutting edge. She might wear a leopard mini-skirt and long velvet coat. She might deck herself out in silk and feathers. Donna sometimes embarrasses her friends, but secretly they wish they could pull off her dramatic look.

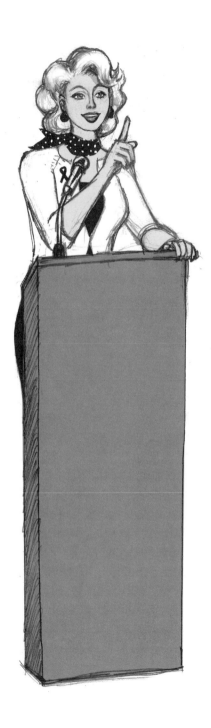

Inside Donna's Closet

Donna is anything but predictable, but whatever she pulls from her closet, all eyes must be on her. Take a peek in Donna's closet; here's what you'll find:

Dramatic jewelry - rings with big stones
Animal anything
Snake and metallic everything
Bold prints and lots of great color
Sunglasses
A fabulous coat that stands alone
Purses (red suede, etc.)
Capes
Fur trims
Baubles, beads, and bling
Scarves
Fringe
Color! Red, purple, neon, all that glitters

Some of Donna's Favorite Designer's and Labels

All the big brands have something for Donna. In fact some of them even have a section of bold, take-notice styles that are right up Donna's alley. Whether Donna is shopping at garage sales, resale shops and discount marts, or high-end department stores and specialty boutiques, Donna makes a bee line for the most dramatic, eye-catching thing in the store. It doesn't matter where she shops, as long as she finds something that makes an impression. When she does browse the name brands, however, here are some of her favorite designs:

Surrealist   *Boho Chic*
Babette   *Mesmerize*
Alberto Makali   *Joseph Ribkoff*
Nanette Lapore   *Lunaluze*
Diane VonFurstenberg   *Nicole Miller Scarves*

 ## Famous Donnas

Do you recognize Donna in any of these famous women?

Bette Midler   *Kathy Griffin*
Missy Elliot   *Kristie Alley*
Tina Turner   *Sarah Silverman*
Cher   *Paula Deen*
Christina Aguilera   *Pink*
Danica Patrick   *Lady GaGa*
Fergie   *Queen Latifah*
Jenny McArthy   *Robin Meade*
Joss Stone   *Jennifer Lopez*

 ## On Donna's Bookshelf

What's Donna reading these days? Anything that will get her noticed, whether it is the latest from the branding gurus, tips on getting noticed, or profiles of folks out there who are as brazen as she is. And while we're pretty sure she'd rather be out getting herself noticed than reading about being out, here are a couple of books you may find on her shelf:

- *Rules for Renegades*, by Christine Comaford-Lynch
- *Kiss My Tiara*, by Susan Jane Gilman

- *The Magic of Thinking Big*, by David Schwartz
- *Brazen Careerist*, by Penelope Trunk
- *How to Swim with the Sharks Without Being Eaten Alive*, by Harvey Mackay
- *Brag! The Art of Tooting Your Horn-Without Blowing It*, by Peggy Klause
- *Power Networking*, by Donna Fisher
- *Confessions of Shameless Self Promoters*, by Debbie Allen
- *Tipping Point, Blink* and *Outliers*, by Malcolm Gladwell
- *Never Eat Alone*, by Keith Ferrazzi
- *The Bad Girl's Guide to Getting What You Want*, and other title and finds by Cameron Tuttle

Movies On Donna's Netflix Queue

Chicago	*Moonstruck*
My Big, Fat Greek Wedding	*Almost Famous*
A Star is Born	*Frida*
Desperately Seeking Susan	*Beaches*
Dreamgirls	*A Fish Called Wanda*
First Wives' Club	*Thelma and Louise*
Pirates of the Caribbean	*The Turning Point*
Election	*Gloria*
Hairspray	*Kill Bill, Vol. 1 & 2*
Something Wild	*Private Benjamin*
Priscilla Queen of the Desert	

The Importance of Being Donna:
Out on the Town: Get Donna-tude!

Okay, it's true. While you may need to call on Donna to rock you through the workday or into a brilliant new career, dressing like Donna on the job or at the interview may not be the best career move, depending on the job in question. Still, what is the point of having Donna's wildly outlandish, bold, and colorful wardrobe if you aren't going to use it?

It's time to take Donna to town. Get a little crazy, because not only does Donna dress wild, she *is* wild. Whether she is donning a wig, a feather boa, or a big red lipstick smile, she can come up with a party things-to-do list that you never even dreamed of. Donna is the girl to call when you want to try something silly, outrageous or just plain fun. She will get you noticed, and will have a ball doing it!

But when you take Donna out on the town, there is one part of her you can leave at the office – the tooting. Yes, tooting your horn and selling your personal brand may be just what is needed when career confidence is the game of the day, but with your girlfriends, you can leave the bragging, the spreading the word of your good deeds, and personal PR firm behind. Your friends don't need to hear how great you are, trust us, they already know.

"I'm tough, I'm ambitious, and I know exactly what I want. If that makes me a bitch, okay."

Madonna

*"We must be willing to let go of the life
we have planned, so as to have the life that is
waiting for us."*

Joseph Campbell

CHAPTER FIVE

Hanging Out
Hanna

Is There a Little Hanna in You?

☐ Sleeping in past noon is a luxury that I relish.

☐ Sure, I procrastinate. Sue me.

☐ I love listening to the sound of rain outside my window. Those are the days when I can just lay around in my comfy clothes and read.

☐ Hair is not meant for everyday washing. That's what baseball caps were made for. (Makeup is overrated too.)

☐ I love to snuggle with my down comforter to watch TV, read a book, flip through a magazine, or take a delicious nap.

☐ I enjoy buying stationary and cards, but often forget to send the outgoing mail.

☐ There is a huge collection of t-shirts stuffed in my dresser drawers.

☐ I love sweats, pull-on flannel pants, boxers, and yoga bottoms - the more comfortable, the better.

☐ There are stacks of magazines, books, and mail scattered throughout my house.

☐ On days that I do not have to go out, I don't. On those days, I may not change out of my jammies until around 4 p.m. ... if at all.

Who is Hanna ?

Hanna is the one who knows when it's time to charge our batteries.

Some days you just need a whole lot of nothing. No work to do. No errands to run. No hair to brush. These are the days when the thought of writing a status report seems daunting. When going out for a run feels laughable. When the suggestion of even getting a pedicure sounds downright exhausting.

These are the days that are made for Hanna, Queen of Comfort. Some folks may call her lazy, but Hanna will tell you is there is something genuinely rewarding, ultimately gratifying, and deviously glorious about just doing nothing every once in a while.

Hanna has perfected the art of hanging out. In the world according to Hanna, her day may go something like this:

The alarm sounds at 6 a.m. (obviously set for Kate). She hits snooze for about an hour and a half until she finally turns off the alarm altogether and settles back under the covers to enjoy the rest of her beauty sleep. Finally managing to roll out of bed at 11:30 a.m., she drags the blankets with her as she reaches for her favorite book, a couple of magazines, her journal, and a bowl of popcorn. She heads straight for the couch and burrows down for an afternoon of blissful nothingness.

The phone rings. Once. Twice. It seems like nobody is home. Three times. Four. Look carefully and you may see a bulge under the pile of blankets on the couch. Five times. Then silence. Whoever was calling has given up, and the bulge under the couch breathes a sigh of relief. A hand shoots out from under the blankets, reaches for the cell phone to check the messages. She may not want to talk right now, but that doesn't mean she's not curious, and maybe a little happy you called.

Hanna is tired. She needs a break from all the noise, commotion, and demands of everyday life. Hanna is the one who looks at the clock at 4 p.m. and realizes that she hasn't taken a shower yet. She has no problem calling in sick when she is in the middle of a great book, which she just can't bear to put down. Hanna simply refuses to get dressed up and put on makeup unless she has to. She is low-key, down to earth, and filled with creative potential. She only needs a short break to wake up the inspired genius that lurks beneath her surface.

On those rare occasions when she finds the strength to drag herself away from quality "couch time," she may suggest spending the whole day walking around a downtown art festival, enjoying an outdoor concert series, or doing anything that will kill the whole day, as long as she doesn't have to do the planning or driving. Hanna is the one to call if you need to escape to the beach. She doesn't need a rainy day to go to a movie. She is the girl in the corner of the coffee shop who has been there for four hours with her nose in a book, sipping the same cup of java. She's a brilliant and avid knitter, when she feels like it.

Hanna's favorite words are unwind, lay back, slow down and *chillax* (a subtle combination of chill and relax). She is the sovereign ruler of procrastination, the master of nap taking, quite creative when it comes to yawning, and simply marvelous at waiting around for nothing to happen. In this time of over-scheduling, BlackBerrys, iPhones, and rushing about, Hanna simply stops.

If she has to she will run out to buy a bottle of Pinot, but if you see her in the store, don't bother to say hello. She is on a secret mission and will not allow anyone to distract her from her goal of high-powered lounging.

Hanna believes that when things get rough, the best gift that you can give yourself is permission to take a personal time-out. That means that if you have had a tough week at work, take a break before you get back in there; or if you have had an emotionally draining encounter, recognize the effort expended and let it go.

Too often we push and push.

We think, "If I just put in one more hour, one more day, one more week, I can get through this."

We forget that if we exhaust all of our inner resources, then we won't have anything left with which to face the world. It is at this point that Zoë may remind us to go for a run or to a yoga class, but even those rejuvenating activities may be too much effort for Hanna. Hanna will remind you that it takes effort to put on running shoes, or that you can't do yoga if you can't be bothered to get yourself to the mat. There is a significant difference between conscious relaxation and just hanging out. And Hanna won't let anyone tell you differently.

It is during this down time that Hanna helps bring some of our best ideas to light. She knows that when we free up our minds from all the daily clutter, there is suddenly room for creativity and vision. In this state, we might see something in a magazine or on TV that sparks a moment of creative genius.

Our challenge with Hanna is pulling ourselves out of our nothing-ness haze to actually do something with those brilliant ideas. But we've got Donna for that.

Hanna Values: *The Joy of Nothingness*

In a society that puts tremendous value on keeping busy and being successful, Hanna has the courage to go against the grain and place value on just doing nothing. It's not that she's lazy, but she has the strength to just say no, to reboot her internal computer and allow herself the sweet joy of getting her creative juices flowing.

Hanna's Core Values:

Alone Time
"Control-Alt-Delete" / "ForceQuit"
> *(she doesn't PC/Mac discriminate)*
Courage
Creativity
Freedom
Pleasure
Questioning
Rebelliousness
Self-Preservation
Stillness

Perception Is Reality

At first blush, it may be tempting to write Hanna off – what does she do anyway? On the surface she may seem vacant and out-of-it, but go a little deeper and you may catch a glimpse of her glory before she nods off for yet another nap.

Hanna Idealized	Hanna Misunderstood
Independent	*Detached*
Comfortable	*Sloppy*
Dreamy	*Irresponsible*
Down to Earth	*Spacey*
Cozy	*Couch Potato*
Carefree	*Slacker*
Free	*Flakey*
Takes care of herself	*Selfish*
Laid Back	*Lazy*
Lets it all go	*Never gets it done*

When Do You Need Hanna?

We don't usually want to admit that we need Hanna, but when our pace gets a little too fast and our world gets a little too crazy, she's a good friend to have. However, we often call on Hanna when it's already too late – when we've drawn the last straw, when we desperately need to recharge. But if we aren't careful, we can get lost in her Nothing-Nothing Land and instead of recharging the batteries, we just power down completely. The trick with Hanna is calling on her in the nick of time – appreciating her while she is hanging around, and knowing when it is time for her to go home.

Go on, admit it. You need Hanna:

- When you have a three-day weekend with nothing planned
- On a rainy Sunday
- When you need to take a "mental-health" day
- After a week of relatives visiting
- Before you begin a new job
- When you have an impossible work schedule and are ready to lose it
- When you are feeling over-scheduled and need a rest
- After a long week of work when you desperately need sleep
- When your favorite author's soon-to-be bestseller comes out
- When there is a *Law and Order* marathon on TNT (ok, fine, there's always a *Law and Order* marathon on, so insert your own favorite television marathon here)

Top 10 Tips *from Hanna*
on how to "do nothing" well

Hanging out with Hanna requires a bit of awareness and concentration to balance between extremes. Of course, awareness and concentration can be a challenge to achieve when you are truly doing nothing. Here are a couple of quick tips from H-girl:

1. *Don't let routine run your life.* No matter how constructive the pursuit, compulsion can become toxic.

For example, exercise is wonderful and a regular regimen is great, but you can always take a couple of days off without considering it a sin.

2. *Silence is Golden.* You don't have to talk to be an active participant in life. Listening may very well be a lost art.

3. *Cancel something.* Don't waste time looking for an excuse. Just say no.

4. *Tune out the "noise."* That is, let go of other people's opinions.

5. *Don't ignore the muse.* Inspiration can come at the most inconvenient times. If doing nothing stirs up your creative side, capture your gem in a journal or recording. Just because you are taking it easy doesn't mean you need to let genius pass you by.

6. *Listen to your body.* Chances are it will let you know when you need a rest.

7. *Order in.* Keep your favorite menus by the phone or bookmarked on your computer so you don't need to rummage around when the time comes.

8. *Let it ring.* When you take "me time," really take it. Take a hot bath, listen to music, read a book, close your eyes – but whatever you do, don't answer that phone.

9. *Make your bed.* Then lie in it. Buy top of the line organic cotton sheets with a great thread count (okay, that tip comes from Kate, but believe me, Hanna will thank you for it!) Although to be thoroughly loungy, Hanna will need a great down comforter, afghan, cashmere, or other killer soft blanket and luxurious pillows (truth be told, if she had money to burn, she'd head to the downtown Westin Hotel and hide away for the day buried in a "Heavenly Bed").

10. *Practice daytime napping.* Once you have the comfy bed ready, Hanna says jump in. Whether you are going for a quick nod or a real doozie that puts you out for a while, Hanna is pro-nap and she swears by putting the power in power nap. But Hanna wants you to respect the process, so here are her steps to nappy goodness:

- Draw the blinds and make it as dark as possible
- Take off any constricting clothing and of course your shoes
- Set your cell phone for your wake-up time
- Get under the covers
- Close your eyes and let go – forget counting sheep, even if you don't think you are sleeping, let your mind go and enjoy the rest

Try to refrain from pulling a "Costanza," that is, a mini-nap under the desk at work … unless the conditions are just right and proper precautions have been taken.

"After all, computers crash, people die, relationships fall apart. The best we can do is breathe and reboot." [8]

Carrie Bradshaw, *Sex in the City*

Dressing *with Hanna*
Hanna knows how to make it work with "Shabby Chic"

As you may have guessed, Hanna's style is unstructured and comfortable. Take a peek in Hanna's closet. Don't be scared. Those piles won't bite. Go a little closer – here's what you'll find:

Comfortable clothes, like pull-on pants & oversized tees
Baggy jeans
Baseball caps
Elastic
Tennis shoes
Flip flops
Cargo shorts
Lots of pajamas
Slippers
Terry cloth robe

 ## Point and Click: Where to Shop for Hanna

While her clothing choices typically include an over-abundance of comfortable clothes she can lounge around in, that doesn't mean Hanna doesn't enjoy shopping. She just prefers to do all of her shopping online …   preferably from bed. Lucky for Hanna, the increased availability of just about anything you could ever want via the Internet makes this an easy habit to appease.

To keep it simple, let's focus on those loungy-basics. Here are some websites that help fill Hanna's closet and promise to help keep her under the covers a little while longer:

PajamaMania.com
hipundies.com
sleepyheads.com
michaelstars.com
threedots.com
thecatspjs.com
karenneuburger.com

Freshpair.com
Zappos.com
AmericanApparel.net
PhysiciansFormula.com
Aveda.com
Origins.com
barenecessities.com

Famous Hannas

Do you recognize Hanna in any of these famous women? It may be hard to tell since most of us tend to keep our Hanna's hidden, but we have a hunch that these lovelies may be down-to-earth enough to go ultra-casual, free enough to just chill out, and smart enough to know when it is time to recharge that creative energy we all love. Plus, we just want an excuse to hang out with these could-be Hannas.

Alyson Hannigan
Christina Applegate
Drew Barrymore
Emma Watson
America Ferrera
Lauren Graham
Norah Jones
Parker Posey

Sandra Bullock
Tina Fey
Ellen DeGeneres
Amanda Bynes
Amy Poehler
Maggie Gyllenhaal
Mary-Louise Parker
Rosie O'Donnell

Hanna's Bookshelf

Hanna's bookshelf (coffee table, floor, you name it) is filled with books she's gobbled up and quite a few that she just hasn't gotten around to yet. Hanna loves fiction – titles that were recommended to her, and those that looked interesting as she browsed the shelves. With no genre-bias, she'll read anything from the classics to the up-and-comers, from romance to mystery, from chic lit to frat humor. Leave the short stories to Kate to read on her commute or in between appointments, Hanna is addicted to the serials that will keep her going for a while – and although she's not above keeping up with the kids (think *Harry Potter* and *Twilight*) – we have seen her with a literary award-winner or two.

Still, there are a few books out there that are geared towards helping us bring out our inner Hanna. Some of those include:

- *Culinarytherapy: The Girl's Guide to Food for Every Mood,* by Beverly West (specifically the chapters: "When You're Hungry For Love: Comfort Food" and "When You're a Couch Potato: Your Inner Guy Food." Pure Hanna.)
- *Don't Sweat the Small Stuff - and It's All Small Stuff,* by Richard Carlson
- *Living the Simple Life,* by Elaine St. James
- *Make Your Creative Dreams Real: A Plan for Procrastinators, Perfectionists, Busy People, and People Who Would Really Rather Sleep All Day,* by SARK (actually, anything by SARK, let your creativity play)
- *Nothing To Do, Nowhere To Go: Waking Up To Who You Are,* by Thich Nhat Hanh
- *Simple Abundance,* by Sarah Ban Breathnach
- *Take a Nap, Change Your Life*, by Sara Mednick and Mark Ehrman
- *Stitch 'N Bitch: The Knitter's Handbook,* by Debbie Stoller
- *The Art of Doing Nothing: Simple Ways to Make Time for Yourself,* by Veronique Vienne and Erica Lennard

Movies In Hanna's Netflix Queue: Bring her the popcorn and she'll never leave the house

We have already discussed how the Internet has made shopping easier for Hanna, but that modern miracle has given Hanna yet another excuse to stay glued to the couch – the hits just keep on coming. Netflix was made for Hanna. Now with Blockbuster following the send-it-to-your-door trend and media from iTunes, Hulu, and other sources that allow for legal watching and downloading, there is no excuse for missing out on pop-culture eye-candy on the small screen. By the time this goes to print, you will probably be able to just think of a movie or television episode and will it to your door, but not just yet.

Honestly, Hanna likes too many movies to count, not to mention seasons upon seasons of network and cable television broadcasts. But, if we must name a few flicks for a rainy day, here is handful of random Hanna favorites that she could watch over and over and over:

Annie Hall	*Philadelphia Story*
Back to the Future	*Princess Bride*
Sunset Boulevard	*The Usual Suspects*
Office Space	*Wedding Crashers*
Chinatown	*Shrek*
Dazed and Confused	*Singles*
Godfather (all of them)	*Sixteen Candles*
Casablanca	*The Big Lebowski*
Groundhog Day	*Ferris Bueller's Day Off*
There's Something About Mary	*Better Off Dead*
Star Wars Trilogy	*Knocked Up*
Gentlemen Prefer Blondes	*Rear Window*

"Never eat anything at one sitting that
you can't lift."

Miss Piggy

Comfort *Foods*

Hanna loves her comfort foods. Comfort foods go perfectly with laying around doing nothing. They play an important part of her life. These are the foods that trigger good feelings tied into memories and nostalgia, like macaroni and cheese, grilled cheese (anything cheesy!), popcorn, and chocolate. Comfort foods have a direct line to our emotions. They connect us back to feelings and experiences that we had when we were younger.

According to some experts, men and women supposedly have different comfort food lists. Men find comfort in foods associated with meals prepared for them by their mothers, like mashed potatoes, meat loaf, and pasta. Women, on the other hand, usually do not find comfort in preparing their foods. They would rather rip into a bag of cookies, Cheetos, chips, Twizzlers, or popcorn, or order their comfort foods out, no matter how easy the prep would be – watch out Rachel Ray! Ordering plain old grilled cheese at a restaurant is a classic Hanna move.

Hanna will tell you that the comfort foods we crave have a lot to do with the mood that we are in. You might crave a pepperoni pizza when you're happy, hot chocolate when you're blue, and a bag of greasy potato chips when you're bored. Name your mood and name your food.

"Sitting quietly, doing nothing, spring comes, and the grass grows by itself."

Zen Proverb

"The fountain of youth is in your mind, your talents, the creativity you bring to your life and the lives of the people you love. When you learn to tap this source you will truly have defeated age."

Sophia Loren

CHAPTER SIX

Trendy
Trudy

Is There a Little Trudy in You?

☐ I am upbeat, optimistic, and energetic. I enjoy life and every day just keeps getting better.

☐ The *Dancing With the Stars* folks have nothing on me. I watch all their moves, practice in my living room and am not afraid to shake my booty. Laughing helps.

☐ I am addicted to flipping through magazines. I scan through everything from *InStyle* and *Elle* to *Time* and *The Economist*. I like *Fast Company*, *Wired*, and *Page Six*.

☐ I have the latest hairstyle and I get highlights and color even if I don't have to hide the gray.

☐ I am open to change and stay current with technology. I have been known to blog, tweet and post to Flickr.

☐ I can't wait to start all the fun projects on my to-do list. I may not finish them all, but getting things kicked off is half the fun!

☐ I go to the movies and have seen almost every movie nominated for an award, not to mention some indies that no one has even heard of yet.

☐ I enjoy going to new or exotic restaurants, where I relish trying different things.

☐ I watch my favorite TV shows and clips on Hulu.

☐ I stopped leaving phone messages. If I can't reach you I'll simply text you and it's done.

Who is Trudy ?

Trudy is the ageless spirit that keeps us young and with it.

Trudy always knows what's up. The latest music? She's heard it. The latest celebrity gossip? She knows it. The latest fashion accessory? She blogged about it before anyone even knew that it was hot.

Her radar for tuning into trends is always right on.

Trudy has read books before Oprah, eaten cupcakes from Magnolia Bakery before Carrie and the girls made them a West Village tourist stop, listened to Outkast before Andre 3000 tried his hand at acting, and knew when to turn in her Kate Spade for a Tory Burch.

Chances are that by the time you read this, everything in this wannabe-hipster chapter will be so ten days ago. Rest assured, though, Trudy saw the coming of each demise, and long before Heidi Klum could tell us *"auf wiedersehen,"* Trudy had already moved on to the next big thing.

Trudy was there when my 80-year-old grandmother asked for a Coach bag for Christmas. She was with my 60-year-old friend when she first saw the "Lazy Sunday" digital short on *Saturday Night Live* (the *Chronicles of Narnia* rap) and started emailing the YouTube clip to everyone she knew. She is with every 16 to 22-year-old who ever tried on "this" with "that" and thought, "Hey, it just might work."

Whatever it is you need, Trudy knows where to get it. And not just the high dollar designer stuff either (although she sure likes the real stuff when her budget allows for it). She can shop at Target just as effortlessly as Saks. She is as comfortable in TJMaxx and Marshall's as she is at Nordstrom and that trendy little second-hand shop in the cool part of town. Call it a gift, but Trudy can find top notch steals just about anywhere, including the fancy department stores, outlet malls, discount stores, online, or from street vendors.

But Trudy is not just about Ugg Boots and Ugly Dolls. She is more than chandelier earrings, the blogosphere, podcasts, and Apple-anything. Sure, she has seen the latest clips and movies, downloaded the hottest tunes, eaten at the hippest restaurants, and sipped on the most outrageous martini concoctions. But Trudy knows that being trendy is more than just about being cool. Trudy keeps it real, because she is young at heart. She listens to the word on the street. She keeps an open mind and explores all new possibilities. Rather than just following trends, she leads the way and creates new ones.

Trudy sees life as an adventure, and she wants to take you with her. She has an insatiable curiosity that pushes her to see things as interesting rather than different. She embraces diversity and new thought. She likes to mix things up and try things out.

She is a great friend to knock ideas around with because she is a thrill-seeker and an innovator. And when you are around her, you want to seek and invent too. Trudy's mind is continually stimulated by what surrounds her. She leverages her ideas and energy from what's happening on her block and around the world. But Trudy knows she can keep up with all the latest trends and still be irrelevant. So she pushes herself to let go of the old clothes, ideas, and even people who are holding her back. Trudy sees a world of neverending possibilities, and is open to reinvention and learning of all kinds. She dreams up the cleverest of schemes and then works with you to make those dreams come to life.

Trudy knows that her age does not define her. As Trudy gets older, her confidence, self-esteem, and self-knowledge grow with her. Trudy's vast experiences give her the confidence to try new things without getting hung-up on what others may think. She strives to have fun, stay young and, most of all, celebrate every day she is alive.

 ## Trudy's Values: A Curious Mind

Trudy is the playful and rebellious teenager that lives inside each of us (minus the sullen attitude and bad acne.) Her upbeat attitude keeps us young and alive. She is our very own change agent who is willing to let go of what is old, outdated or no longer necessary in order to make room for the new, innovative, and whatever it is we really need to take our groove to the next level.

Trudy embraces diversity and change. Her natural curiosity allows her to be open to adventure as she explores all things new and shiny. As she gets older, Trudy refuses to act her age. She continues to push boundaries, learn new lessons ,and keep her body, mind and spirit young and full of life.

Trudy's Core Values:

Change
Creativity
Curiosity
Diversity
Flexibility
Innovation
Learning
Open-mindedness
Positive attitude
Youthful thinking

Perception is Reality

Trudy is not afraid of change. She is not afraid to go out on a limb to try something before anyone else has dared to think of it. She is not afraid to be the coolest kid in school. Actually, she loves it, she craves it…all of it. Trudy is always on the lookout for something newer, something cooler, something better. It is the spark that gives her energy, retains her youth, and keeps her going at full throttle.

While this makes her an exciting force to reckon with, it can also be a little, well, exhausting. She is always moving, always playing, always wanting more. It's enough to make the Kate in us to wonder, "Why all the fuss? Why can't we just stay where we are – maybe a little more traditional, a little more tried and true, a little more… normal?"

Trudy at her best helps us test our boundaries and embrace the exuberant joys of youth – she wants to keep us fresh, innovative, and alive. Still, even Trudy knows that she needs to be careful of change for change's sake alone. Her challenge is to remain open to endless possibilities, while staying true to her own inner voice. Of course, if that inner voice is telling her to be the coolest kid in school, why fight it?

Trudy Idealized	Trudy Misunderstood
Hip and "with-it"	*Hipper-than-thou*
Energetic	*ADHD/Hyper*
Cool	*Immature*
Innovative genius	*Self-absorbed*
Youthful	*Juvenile*
Open to what comes her way	*Ridiculous*
Positive	*Dreamer*
Flexible	*Chameleon*
Enthusiastic	*Superficial*
Expert Shopper	*Spendthrift*

When Do You Need Trudy?

Trudy never looks more appealing than when you are stuck in a rut or bored with your everyday routine. She teases us with the next best thing in electronics. She laughs when we roll our eyes and mutter, "these kids today."

In our fast paced world, Trudy helps us navigate between the changes that we need which give us life, and those we need to let go of which drag us down. She helps us keep our minds open and our youthful spirit fully charged. Whether you are a grandmother texting your 8-year-old grandson, Baby Boomer manager baffled by the latest crop of Generation "Y" new hires, or just a smart woman trying to stay current, you need the Trudy mindset to get you through and keep your motor running.

Here are a few situations when you especially need Trudy:

- When you need to reinvent yourself
- When you are deciding what shade to color your hair
- When you feel challenged (even daunted) by technology
- When you are thinking about making a change - moving, getting a new look, or switching jobs or careers
- When your kids keep begging for a new cell phone
- When you post to your Facebook profile
- Christmas shopping for your nieces and nephews
- When teaching your parents how to Skype so they can see your kids when they call
- When you are bored and tired of your routine
- On vacation or during the holidays
- Shopping for clothes and make-up
- Cleaning out your closet
- Out for fun, looking for a movie, hip new café, restaurant, bookstore or party spot
- When you are ready to start blogging
- Eating oysters - okay, swallowing oysters!
- Brainstorming
- Most of all...anytime you bore yourself

"And now, I'm just trying to change the world, one sequin at a time."

Lady Gaga

Top 10 Tips *from Trudy*
Because Change is Good

Trudy encourages us to embrace the fast-talking, pop-reference-filled world of hipster goodness, and she is full of big energy and new ideas to help us get there. For those of us who are a little reluctant to dive in headfirst, she promotes taking it slow: start by mixing things up, look for a fresh new take on your surroundings, and seek new activities to introduce into your life. It may be as small as just changing the channel, surfing the web for this week's buzz, or taking a Jazzercise class to workout to the latest hits. (Yes, we said Jazzercise. If you haven't been to class since the 1980s, you are in for a pleasant surprise!)

But for those of us with a more adventurous side, Trudy can't wait to get her hands on us! There are millions of ways to stay young and relevant, but staying ahead of the curve? Now, that's Trudy's specialty. Trudy is often asked how she stays so current, how she knows things before anyone else has even heard of them, how she stays so incredibly cool. It is a good thing for us that she loves to share her secrets, and she even created a cheat-sheet for us.

1. *Find high fashion without the guilt, shop Gilt.com.* For an online luxury retailer, The Gilt Group gives an amazing 70% discount. Gilt plays to Trudy's thrill-seeking nature by posting sales from top designers every day, precisely at noon, and taking them down 36 hours later. If you snooze you lose because many of the "cool" items sell out in the first few hours! You have to be a member to buy, so If you want to join (for free), email us and we will send you an invitation.

2. *Turn the music up, even at your desktop.* Trudy loves her *tuneage* and she uses streaming music sites to keep her up-to-date on the latest music trends. There are so many sites to choose from, but Trudy's favorite is Pandora. To use Pandora, type in the name of a favorite artist or song and the site will automatically generate a continuously updating playlist of stylistically similar tracks. Other websites that build personal playlists and share the *music love* include Lala, Grooveshark, and divShare.

3. *Huff and puff.* How does Trudy stay so current? Each morning she spends about five minutes reading the headlines on the *Huffington Post* (occasionally balancing it out with a glance a the *Drudge Report*). The site brings together news, blogs, and original content to cover politics, media, business, style, world news, comedy, and even the green movement. We also love that *HuffPo* co-founder Arianna Huffington was named number 12 in *Forbes* magazine's first-ever list of the "Most Influential Women In Media" in 2009.

4. *What's happening, hot stuff?* When Trudy wants to go a little deeper on a topic, she goes to her own personal researcher, a website called Alltop. As the name suggests, Alltop helps readers keep on top of all items of interest. Alltop collects the headlines of the latest stories from the best sites and blogs that cover a topic.

5. *Write your own material.* Long before *Julie and Julia* became a best-selling book and a major motion picture, Trudy was following Julie Powell on Salon. Back when Julie was a self-proclaimed "government drone" she took on the momentous task of cooking her way through Julia Child's *Mastering the Art of French Cooking* and documenting her year-long efforts for all of the *www* to see. Inspired, Trudy started a little blogging of her own. Blogging keeps Trudy's writing skills sharp, her humor finely tuned and her trend-seeking honest as she teams up with Donna to speak (or write) her mind *(www.thesevenwomenproject.com)*.

6. ***Get out of town.*** Trudy stays young by travelling as often as possible, and she begs us all to take a *real* yearly vacation. A study by the State University of New York, Oswego, published in 2000, found that people who take a real vacation at least once a year are almost 30% less likely to die of a heart attack during the next decade. Get out, explore and have fun. Here's how to vaca ("*vay-cay*") Trudy-style:

• ***Get going.*** Trudy loves the accessibility of travel sites like Kayak. With an abundance of pricing and schedules for her travel needs, Trudy can look for something specific, or leave it to the travel gods to find her a new adventure.

• ***Get connected.*** Trudy found a free web-tool at TripIt that organizes her travel into a master online itinerary, and then links up with other social media to let Trudy's friends know she's on her way.

• ***Get the app for that.*** Trudy uses her iPhone's favorite *app*, FlightTrack Pro to stay on top of things once the adventure begins. It syncs with TripIt to keep track of her flight status, advise her of gate changes, and alert her to weather delays.

7. *Sit at the kids table.* When Trudy is really looking for a good pop culture scoop, she steps away from the blogs and the magazines and calls upon her secret weapon…her 14-year old niece. You can too, for that matter. Any *'tween* in your family or circle of friends will do. But you better contact them on Facebook or with a text message, otherwise you'll never reach them.

8. *Say "Yes!" before you say "No."* Try something you have never done before or something that you would typically reject because it sounds silly, immature, crazy, or just so not you. When you play with your boundaries, you may find something new or innovative that is worth saying "yes" to. Of course, you may validate your "no," but at least you'll know you gave it a shot.

9. *Age gracefully.* If you have an older friend and you like the way she is aging, ask her to share her secrets. If you are that older friend, embrace your age with elegance and then share about it. As Liz Lemon on 30 Rock said, "You can be Meryl or Madonna, it's your choice."

10. *Start your own trend.* Rather than only following trends that other people set, Trudy leads the way and creates new ones. She reminds us that at some point you are going to have to go out on a limb. Put all those creative juices to work and make something happen. Soon people will be following you!

Dressing *with Trudy*
Trudy knows how to stay current at any age.

Trudy's style is current. She is a trend-setter and a *fashionista*. Trudy knows that not all trends are for her, so she continually sharpens her keen eye. She patiently tries all kinds of new styles and continues to edit her own wardrobe, especially when she is shopping.

And Trudy is quite the shopper! Because Trudy stays current on all the latest fashions, she has developed the "Fashion 6th Sense" and can spot a real bargain a mile away. If you do your fashion homework you too will develop "the Eye" and be able spot a great bargain anywhere.

Trudy advises us not to spend lots of money on your trendy items. Invest in the great basics and add the drama with the trends and color! Get to know the off-beat designers that are off-price and affordable.

To make sure there is always room in Trudy's closet for the latest got-to-have-it item, Trudy attacks her wardrobe in three easy steps: Release, Restock, Repeat.

Step One: Release or "The Art of Letting Go"

Unlike fine wine, your clothes do not get better with age. In fact, when you wear outdated or ill-fitting clothes you open yourself up to looking older, dated, and even frumpy. Trudy wants you to live in the moment and be honest with yourself. When you are willing to let go of what used to work to make room for what will work now, it is a powerful change. Think about old clothing the same way you think about old ideas. Trudy tells you to let them go.

Now is the time to go through your closet and your drawers and ask yourself, "What have I not worn for the past two years and why haven't I worn it?" Maybe it never fit quite right, or you have gained or lost a few pounds. Maybe it's not really you or who you think you are. Maybe you think you look bad in it or it is outdated.

For whatever reason, it's time to get it out of your closet. You may choose to store these garments in boxes for a while and let them multiply under your bed, but get them out of your closet. They are confusing you. Nina Garcia, the fashion director of *Elle* magazine, writes in *The Little Black Book of Style*, that each of us needs to become a fashion editor and throw out the items that we don't wear and that don't look good on us.

Step Two: Restock – Places you might find Trudy Shopping

Now that you've cleaned out your closet, it's time to start replacing some of those discarded clothes. Try to add at least three new basic clothing items to your wardrobe each season (think Kate) and one trendy piece (think Trudy). Again, you don't have to spend a fortune to look current. Reading magazines and cruising the fashion blogs and websites will give you the knowledge and the Trudy Eye for what's in this season. Once you know what you are looking for you, like Trudy, you will be able to spot it at any price.

Some of Trudy's Favorite Places to Shop Include:

Black and White	*Zara*
Very Vera Wang for Kohl's	*H&M*
Kate Moss for the Top Shop	*Loehmans*
Macy's I.N.C. department	*Sephora*
Nicole Miller for JCPenny	*Etui*
It's All About You, Kirkwood	*Target*
Saks and Saks Off Fifth	*DSW*
Anthropologie	*Century 21*

Support your favorite small boutiques in your area. Get to know the owner and develop a great relationship so that she knows you, your taste and your body.

Step Three: Repeat … again and again

Trudy won't stand for stagnation. While it may feel like quite an accomplishment the first time you get through Steps One and Two, Trudy is clear that you can't stop there. She is constantly scanning her wardrobe for update opportunities. She makes ongoing assessments of her closet to edit out what no longer works and add in just the right pieces she needs to complete her look. Because Trudy knows that what is *fierce* today might be a *hot mess* tomorrow, this is a highly iterative process.

 Famous Trudy's

Trudy is known for trend-setting. Can you guess which trend each of these famous Trudys started? If you need to peek, see page 189 for the answers. [10]

Beyonce	*Carla Bruni Sarkozy*
Katie Holmes	*Diane Keaton*
Jennifer Aniston	*Anne Hathaway*
FarrahFawcett	*Madonna*
Meg Ryan	*Mary Kate Olsen*
Rihanna	
Gwen Stefani	
Cameron Diaz	
Sienna Miller	
Sarah Jessica Parker	

 *Trudy's Bookshelf*

Trudy doesn't think that the only "books" on her shelf should be issues of *Vogue*. In fact, she's not even sure she needs a shelf. Recently, Trudy added a Kindle to her collection of gadgets. Now, in addition to her old school hardcopy reading, she gets her books, magazines, and even an international newspaper or two delivered wirelessly. Whichever format she chooses, some of her favorite books include:

- *What You Wear Can Change Your Life,* by Trinny Woodal & Susannah Constantine
- *Blogging with Moxie,* by Joelle Reeder & Katherine Scoleri
- *Jump Start Your Brain,* by Doug Hall
- *You: Staying Young,* by Michael F. Roizen & Mehmet C. Oz
- *I Feel Bad About My Neck,* by Nora Ephron.
- *A Whole New Mind: Why Right-Brainers Will Rule the Future* and *Drive: The Surprising Truth About What Motivates Us,* by Daniel H. Pink
- *The World is Flat,* by Thomas L. Friedman
- *The Hipsters Handbook,* by Robert Lanhan
- *How Not to Look Old: Fast and Effortless Ways to Look 10 Years Younger, 10 Pounds Lighter, 10 Times Better,* by Charla Krup
- *Blog Blazers,* by Stephane Grenier
- *Younger Next Year: A Guide to Living Like 50 Until You're 80 and Beyond,* by Chris Crowley

Movies In Trudy's Netflix, Hulu and Apple TV Queue:

Trudy's taste in movies tends to skew towards independent, quirky films. She likes to be the first one on the block to see something new. She may not like everything she sees, but she likes to say she saw it. Here are some she loves:

Being John Malkovich　　　　*The Royal Tenenbaums*
(500) Days of Summer　　　　*Heathers*
Amelie　　　　　　　　　　　*Pulp Fiction*
Fantastic Mr. Fox　　　　　　*Ghost World*
Y Tu Mama Tambien　　　　　*Fargo*
Mulholland Drive　　　　　　*Run Lola Run*
Whip It!　　　　　　　　　　*Slumdog Millionaire*
The Science of Sleep　　　　　*Little Miss Sunshine*
Juno
Women on the Verge of a Nervous Breakdown

Trudy *Tweets!*

In order to keep learning and staying young at heart, Trudy turns to the web. While she loves the music, video and endless sources of news she can use, what Trudy finds truly exhilarating is the network. *OMG.* Even though she has heard the tired old argument that no one really cares how many times you had pizza this week, Trudy sees the vast potential in maintaining online connections. When curmudgeons claim the Internet is a huge time-vampire or whine that it is creepy to have total strangers "following" them, Trudy digs in her virtual heels and vigorously defends the value of online sharing.

Trudy shouts it from the mountaintop (or at least posts it in her status): social media is here to stay.

When MySpace came on the scene in 2002 most adults thought that it was just a flashy way for the "kids" to share their photos, music and flaunt their stuff. When Friendster went live the next year, it was just for those nerdy-chic kids who were above it all. When Facebook entered the scene, it was initially for Harvard campus fun. But today, social media has gone from fad to a fundamental shift in the way we communicate and relate to each other. Trudy was there from the beginning, trying out each next great thing. She believes that social media will continue to grow and these tools are destined to play a huge role in our future.

Today, Trudy isn't the only one tapped into the social media landscape through Twitter, Facebook, YouTube, LinkedIn, and blogs galore. Now that these tools are in the mainstream, it's no shocker that Trudy is looking for something new. Today, Trudy and her friends are trying new apps like Foresquare, which lets Trudy leave a trail of virtual breadcrumbs when she is out about town; Blippy, which tracks Trudy's purchases and tells her friends where she got those great suede boots; and Momentoapp that helps Trudy create an online journal, since writing notes to yourself in pen on your body is sooo year 2000. Let us know your faves.

Not only are these tools being used to enhance personal relationships and build virtual community, but they are also great for enhancing business relationships. Social media is quickly becoming part of many business models driving more traffic to blogs and websites.

But for all those cyber-cynics out there, Trudy does have a secret: content matters. If something is really worth saying, say it loud, say it proud, and say it well. Because, really, even Trudy doesn't care how much pizza you ate this week.

"Toughness doesn't have to come in a pinstripe suit."

Dianne Feinstein

CHAPTER SEVEN

Girlie Girl
Gwen

Is There a Little Gwen in You?

- ☐ I love taking the afternoon off and getting a pedicure with my girlfriends.

- ☐ Long or short, I tend to choose skirts and dresses over slacks … unless of course it is a sexy white suit, which is always a girlie-good choice.

- ☐ I am passionate – even emotional. I laugh hard, I cry hard, and I love hard.

- ☐ I value interpersonal relationships and keep my friends close, both male and female.

- ☐ At work I am known as a compassionate leader. I have killer communication skills and am great at pulling together (and keeping together) a cohesive team.

- ☐ I am not afraid to stand up for women. I am strong and sassy, and would never be called a victim.

- ☐ I prefer to sleep in frilly, silky nightwear even when I sleep alone. No baggy college sweats for me.

- ☐ I am proud to look, act, and dress like a radiant woman, whether or not that puts me at an advantage.

- ☐ Whether dressing for work or for kicking around, I take time with my appearance and do not sacrifice my feminine style.

- ☐ My shoes say it all: strappy, sexy, fabulous!

Who is Gwen

Gwen is the strong, radiant, feminine beauty inside each of us.

Gwen is not afraid to show a little skin. She is not afraid to do her hair up right, spray on a little perfume, or even flash a flirty smile that makes the clerk at the grocery store blush.

Gwen loves skirts, ruffles, baubles, lip-gloss, and scented lotions. When Gwen was a little girl she always played "dress-up" in Mom's high heels and a purse. She made a habit of digging into the jewelry drawer and fishing out that long strand of pearls and other tasty treats. Today, Gwen delights in every opportunity she has to play dress-up for real, whether it is a holiday party, a corporate fundraiser, or just a fun night out on the town.

Gwen loves paper dolls and dollhouses, crying at romantic movies, bleaching her hair in the summer, and treating herself to a delicious pedicure. She loves soaking in a bubble bath, not so much to relax like Zoë, but because what girl doesn't get a thrill from swooping her hair up like they do in the movies and getting lost in a big pile of sweet smelling bubbles? As a teen, Gwen was all about slumber parties, toilet papering houses, and making spirit boxes. Even grown-up Gwen still swoons at the mere whiff of getting a valentine or having a secret admirer. Gwen is playful and charming. She loves talking up a storm and interacting with those around her. She is passionate about celebrating all of life's joys and sorrows.

Gwen could be your Aunt Gertrude just as easily as she could be a glamorous movie star. It is the feminine spirit that really moves her, and she just oozes with it.

For some of us, Gwen is one of the more difficult of the seven women to tap into. Somewhere along the way, in our quest to be independent, smart, successful women, many of us bought into the idea that we had to renounce everything in us that makes us feminine. To be strong and taken seriously, we thought we had to put girlie Gwen away.

In the 1980s this meant following the likes of John Malloy and his call for us to "Dress for Success" – which, according to Malloy, meant dressing just like a man, but in clothing lines that attached "Lady" to their brand names. Although business attire for women has softened quite a bit since the days of silk ties and masculine-cut pant suits, the idea that women have to leave their femininity at the door to be successful in the workplace has managed to stick around.

But that is not our Gwen. Our Gwen knows that smart and feminine are not mutually exclusive.

Gwen is not afraid to cry – she just may save it for the safety behind the restroom stall door. In fact, she is not afraid of many of those pesky quirks considered "too girlie." Gwen doesn't buy the idea that there is no time for female frivolity. She is not above showing a wide array of emotions, talking too much, shopping during her lunch hour, or changing her mind. She knows that having pretty nails doesn't slow down her ability to send witty text messages. Or that putting on a party dress doesn't mean she can't hold court in a boardroom.

Successful women have proven that they can still be feminine, thumbing their pretty little noses at negative media images and girls who give girlie a bad name. Gwen embraces her feminine leadership qualities and proves that leading with her heart doesn't hold her back. Rather, leading like a woman makes her a truly transformational leader: creative, inspired, and ready to take on the increasingly complex challenges facing our families, communities, and world.

Our Gwen has found that much needed balance between steadfastness and softness, for she knows that we love her when she is strong and able, and we are proud of her for resisting the urge to resort to a "victim" role.

Gwen is that beautiful knockout inside of you that understands what it takes to have an authentic relationship with both men and women. Gwen represents joyful acceptance of her female attributes and an understanding that in some ways men really are different than we are. She knows the importance of understanding these differences between men and women and celebrating what we share in common. She challenges us to relish the abundance that such diversity inspires. She has stopped battling with men, without stopping the fight for equality all together. Gwen accepts men for who they are and expects the same acceptance from them. She does not want to be a competitor with either sex, believing that it is only through balanced collaboration that true relationships and growth can occur.

Much like Kate, Gwen wants to have it all...and sometimes having it all means showing the world that PINK is not a four-letter word.

Gwen Values: Her Feminine Side

Gwen's values are in line with those attributes that are traditionally considered most feminine. She embraces her feminine spirit and takes heart in those things that bring out her naturally female side. Gwen is drawn to those things in life that enhance her ability to enter into relationship with everything that surrounds her – with people in her life, with the world she lives in, and, perhaps the most intimate relationship of all, with herself.

Gwen's Core Values:

Beauty
Big picture thinking
Collaboration and consensus building
Communication
Emotional connection
Empathy
Integration of work and "real" life
Intuition
Relationship-building
The Divine Feminine

Perception is Reality

If you are more used to Kate's "get-er-done" attitude, Zoë's quest to find meaning in life, or Hanna's laidback style, you might be rolling your eyes at Gwen right now. What's with all those skirts, hair products, and shiny trinkets? I mean, really, who needs the hassle? And could she BE a any more flirtatious? Give me a break. Appreciating Gwen is all about finding a little bit of balance. While the super-girlie Elle Woods may have reminded us that any *Cosmo Girl* knows that the rules of hair care are simple and finite, Gwen never loses sight of the fact that it's her smarts, her heart, and her guts that make her a real woman.

Gwen Idealized	Gwen Misunderstood
Beautiful	Glamazon
Loving/compassionate	Sappy/too Emotional
Understanding	Weak
Healthy body image	Too sexy
Collaborative	Indecisive
Team player	Can't do anything alone
Charming	Airhead
Keen intuition	Lucky
Romantic	Boy crazy
Fabulous feminist	Plays the gender card

When Do You Need Gwen?

In these hard times, it may be easy to dismiss Gwen as trivial or see her ease with making the human connection as superficial. But perhaps it is exactly because life can be tough and meeting new people is harder to do as we get older, that sometimes we need to bring out the softer side of Gwen.

Some days more than others it may be important to our well-being to feel youthful, carefree and pretty ... girlie even. When you want to celebrate being a woman and expressing your feminine side, be sure to bring Gwen:

- When you are tired of wearing pants everywhere you go
- In the summer – it's the right time for girlie sundresses, flowing skirts, and fun sandals
- When you wake up and realize that being right and proper all the time is exhausting…and a little lonely
- Going out on a first date
- When you are put in charge of creating the company's women's initiative programs and mentoring other women
- Dressing up to go out, even if it is to a movie with the girls
- Talking to our daughters and our nieces, or any time we are showing young girls how to love their femininity, have a healthy way of looking at being female, and how not to sell ourselves short or give something up to get others to like us
- At the shoe store, say no to the Naturalizers and yes to strappy goodness
- When you need to remind yourself that you don't have to give up who you are to succeed
- When packing to go on vacation – throw Gwen in the suitcase
- When it's time to stop, collaborate, and listen. You need to get your team to talk to each other and find some common ground
- When you start to doubt yourself and need to remember to trust and follow your instincts. We've all heard the stories of great actors or artists whose teachers told them they would never make it. Follow your gut and remember that success may take a little longer than your planned. Patience, Gwen.

Top 10 Tips *from Gwen:*

Gwen wants you to be a girlie best. She wants you to dress like a girl, think and feel like a girl, and act like a girl. But for Gwen, being girly is not just about how we present ourselves to the world, but also how we express, recognize, and share beauty from the inside out. Gwen's tips are all about bringing this femininity into the spotlight, in some of the obvious ways (put on a dress for heaven's sake!) and some that are just a little more subtle.

1. *Bring sexy back.* Being sexy is more of an attitude than a fashion look. It is more about the twinkle in your eye and your sparkly spirit than a shapely dress and jewels. Stand upright, tall, and open-hearted when you walk into a room. Women who are comfortable in their own skin exude a confidence that tells the world they have value and worth. People are attracted to this confidence, especially if it is pared with approachability and a warm smile.

2. *Hone your emotional intuition.* Women may be stereotypically known for reading more into a situation than is at the surface, but don't take that as a negative. Instead of second guessing yourself all the time, fine tune your emotion barometer to use this power for good. See the subtle details that others might miss, build strong work and personal relationships, listen to verbal and nonverbal cues, and communicate in a insightful but straightforward manner.

3. *Have a good cry.* Know how to read your own emotion levels as well. This isn't to say we need to unleash the tears whenever it suits us or that we should lash out emotionally just because we feel like it, but that we should recognize the very real, very human role that our emotions play in our lives. Back in 2005, *London Times* columnist Helen Rumbelow pointed out the inconsistency that while it seems to be somewhat acceptable (even laudable) for men to throw temper tantrums at work, women crying in public is an emphatic no-no. Take Holly Hunter's character in *Broadcast News*, she is a strong and successful television producer who has periodic, and highly private, cry-breaks before she picks it up and gets back to work. Gwen doesn't want any of us to have to hide our emotional side. Stuffing emotions isn't good for anyone - sometimes we need to let it out. We just need to learn to find the best way to do it.

4. *Set strong boundaries.* Know who you are, what you want, and what you will (and will not) put up with, accept, or be a part of. Start to say "No" when you really are not interested in filling your time with what is being asked of you. Saying no when you mean it makes the "Yes" even more vibrant and meaningful.

5. *Ask for Directions.* Ask for help when you need it. Asking for help doesn't make you look weak; it is all about how you ask. Tap into your collaborative side and recognize the talents and gifts all around you. Gwen knows the importance of building great teams in the workplace, and she sees great value in creating your personal "A Team" at home as well. Seek out what you need and build a help roster. Find a great coach or mentor, a massage therapist, babysitter, some one to help with the cleaning, tailor, dentist, personal physician, and handyman (or woman!).

6. *You can never have too many pair of high heels or good underwear.* It's the little things that can make us feel girlie all over. A great pair of heels does remarkable things to your psyche. It can change your mood, your strut, posture and your attitude about yourself. Heels make a great pair of jeans look even better. But pay as much attention to your lingerie as you do to your shoes. Just because the rest of the world doesn't see it, our unmentionables can go a long way to making us feel mentionably great. Buy your bra and panties to match and while you are at it buy an extra pair of panties and throw out the old, ratty ones. There is nothing worse than the day you get to the bottom of the barrel.

7. *Get rid of toxic people in your life.* Much like old underwear, many women do not like to let go of any relationship, even if it is bad. We are nurturers and we think we can fix it, or we are afraid of hurting someone's feelings. However, some relationships are not worth the effort or the negative effects they have on us. Save your energy for those relationships that bring out the best in both parties.

8. *Talk behind their backs, in a good way.* Women are known for spreading gossip. But as Houston speaker Donna Fisher tells us, make sure that you are known for spreading "good gossip." Spread the word about your co-worker's talent and success. This doesn't take away from your own greatness. Rather, it amplifies it. Instead of talking down about your friends and peers, talking them up makes for a more empowered, more vibrant community that you will all want to be a part of. There is enough room for everyone to shine.

9. *Grow a girl.* The world needs more girlie-girls. Be brave, step up to the plate (any plate!) and bring your sisters with you! Begin to take on leadership roles in your career and your community and encourage your friends and neighbors to join you. Mentor the younger generations and get them on board early. Whether we are teachers, administrators, chiefs, community organizers, executive managers, or volunteers, when women take on leadership roles we tend to make things better. But we need more than a just few of us to lead the way. While we might not agree on everything, as women we tend connect to each other through our shared values and ideas. There is power in numbers.

10. *Think big.* Don't limit yourself to what is right in front of you. Studies show that women tend to take a broader, more holistic view of the world. Dr. Helen Fischer, Biological Anthropologist and research professor at Rutgers University, calls this "web-thinking." We call it awesome. That is, rather than thinking linearly and compartmentalizing data in a left brain manner, women tend to collect lots of information from many different perspectives and put it back together in a new and creative right brain way. To the casual observer, this may seem undisciplined or even scatterbrained. Gwen says that is the ability to see broadly, to integrate various ideas, and even change our minds when we see a new solution. It may be exactly what we need to solve the complex problems of our time.

Dressing *with Gwen*

Gwen believes that professional dress and sensible shoes are stifling the inner woman. Tired of wearing pants everywhere you go? Forget you have legs down there? Gwen wants to help you get ready to let your female essence come alive.

Like her values, Gwen's style is female-focused. She is feminine and flirty. Her style is confident but with soft edges. Sure she has sex appeal, but Gwen's style isn't all about pushing sexy. She's our girlie girl and she has a subtle sexiness and romantic glow.

 ## In Gwen's Closet

Gwen wants to show us how to take the stigma out of going girlie. She is here to dispel the notion that girlie-girls are silly, frivolous, and anti-feminists. Gwen's fashion sense allows you to be feminine and fashionable without compromising your standards.

Gwen loves to wear make-up, jewelry, and fun baubles in her hair. Her fashion vision allows for florals, ruffles, lace, high collars, and soft colors to be incorporated into the new power suit. And let's not forget the number one, true icon of femininity - The Dress. The dress is back, and it's flourishing thanks to our girl Gwen and her girlie sisters everywhere.

Take a peek in Gwen's closet. Here's what you'll find:

- Clothes with a little Lycra so they hold their shape ... and hers
- Soft textures – angora, cashmere, and silk
- Soft colors and tone – light pink, blue, yellow, and lavender
- A white or off-white suit (the most powerfully feminine item in her closet – skirt or pants, it doesn't matter)
- Low-cut neckline on evening wear and bathing suits (picture Susan Sarandon)
- High heels (stilettos, mini-stilettos)
- Silver and gold bustier (to wear under a jacket)
- Black, fitted tuxedo jacket
- Diamond bling (real or cubic zirconium)
- Pencil skirts and A-line dresses
- Cocktail dress ready to go if the situation arises
- Sexy lingerie
- Hairclips and jewelry
- Clutch bag
- A pair of Spanks

Some of Gwen's Favorite Designers and Labels

While Gwen and Trudy share many of the same tastes when it comes to fashion and designers, Trudy will follow just about any cool trend (think Doc Martins and high-top Converse shoes), while Gwen consistently stays more close to her girlie roots (more Manolo Blahniks and L.A.M.B. platform sandals). The following designers and labels are some of Gwen's favorites – especially their dress lines:

Joesph Ribkoff	Nanette Lepore
Linda Segal	BCBG Maxazria
Kay Celine	Tory Burch
Isabel De Pedro	Saint John
Trina Turk	Gucci
David Meister	Diane von Furstenburg

Play Like a Girl

Gwen loves to exercise to stay healthy and to keep her girlish figure. But let's face it, most exercise is anything but ladylike. Enter Nicole DeBoom - or should we say Nicole's da bomb? Nicole is a professional triathlete-turned-entrepreneur with a flair for feminine style. She came up with an idea back in 2003 that women should "never have to sacrifice femininity for performance in their workout clothes." Over the next few years she created a sassy line of kick-butt running and work-out skirts to prove her point. Lucky for Gwen, today a number of more mainstream outfitters (Nike, Brooks, and others) have joined the skirt craze, and the SkirtSport line itself has expanded to include new fitness skirts, dresses, tops and even a "SkirtChaser" fun run series (emphasis on fun).

"There's something so interesting about the combination of vulnerability and being completely in control at the same time. Women should run everything - it's about time."

Jennifer Garner

Do you recognize Gwen in any of these famous women?

Cindy Crawford	January Jones
Kristin Chenoweth	Kristen Bell
Jennifer Hudson	Julia Roberts
Lucy Lawless	Penelope Cruz
Eva Longoria	Lucy Liu
Eva Mendez	Reese Witherspoon
Rosario Dawson	Raquel Welch
Hayden Panettiere	Meghan McCain
Jennifer Garner	Stevie Nicks
Taylor Swift	Sarah Michelle Gellar

 ## Gwen's Bookshelf

Who says girls don't read? Check out some of the titles on Gwen's pretty pink bookshelves:

- *The Bombshell Manual of Style,* by Laren Stover
- *First Sex,* by Helen Fisher
- *The Girl's Guide to Being a Boss (Without Being a Bitch): Valuable Lessons, Smart Suggestions, and True Stories for Succeeding as the Chick-in-Charge,* by Caitlin Friedman and Kimberly Yorio
- *Hip Tranquil Chick,* by Kimberly Wilson (a little Zoë, a little Trudy, but this very pink, very feminine book makes it one of Gwen's top picks)
- *Make a Fortune Selling to Women: The Deal Makers and Deal Breakers You Must Know to Close the Deal Every Time!,* by Connie Podesta

- *Play Like a Man, Win Like a Woman and She Wins, You Win: The Most Important Strategies for Making Women More Powerful,* by Gail Evans
- *Well-Behaved Women Seldom Make History,* by Laurel Thatcher Ulrich
- *Women Lead the Way: Your Guide to Stepping Up to Leadership and Changing the World* by Linda Tarr-Whelan
- *Women at the Top: Powerful Leaders Tell Us How to Combine Work and Family,* by Diane F. Halpern

While Gwen often follows Trudy down the magazine aisles to check out the latest and greatest in women's fashion that the likes of *Vogue, Elle,* and *Glamour* have to offer, over in the pop culture section of the aisle, *Bust* magazine is Gwen's little secret. *Bust*'s tagline claims that it is a magazine "for women who have something to get off their chests" and it's not kidding. The magazine was founded in 1992 by Debbie Stoller and Marcelle Karp and is now owned and run by business partners Stoller and Laurie Henzel. Its pages are chock full of DIY, crafts, music, and a little raciness thrown in for good measure.

"Creating a cultural icon out of some-one who goes, 'I'm stupid, isn't it cute?' makes me want to throw daggers. I want to say to them, 'My grandma did not fight for what she fought for just so you can start telling women it's fun to be stupid. Saying that to young women, little girls, my daughter? It's not okay."

Reese Witherspoon

Movies On Gwen's Netflix Queue

You may have guessed by now that Gwen is a sucker for romantic comedies and chic-flicks that celebrate female friendships. There are a ton out there, but here are some of Gwen's favorites:

13 Going on 30
Bend it Like Beckham
Enchanted
Chocolat
Houseboat
Pretty Woman
Stardust
Say Anything
Legally Blonde
Like Water for Chocolate
Mystic Pizza
The Notebook
Sleepless in Seattle
Sisterhood of the Traveling Pants
Someone Like You
Steel Magnolias
Titanic
Beauty and the Beast
Ten Things I Hate About You
27 Dresses
Miss Congeniality
Twilight
The Princess Diaries
Divine Secrets of the Ya-Ya Sisterhood

Sex in the City
Drop Dead Gorgeous
Sweet Home Alabama
When Harry Met Sally
Clueless
Roman Holiday
Love Story

The Revolution *will not be Televised!*

While we might think of Gwen as a big, glamorous movie star, she has actually been making her mark on the small screen for as long as we remember. True, she has evolved over time (very early versions might have included Laura from the *"Dick Van Dyke Show"*) and she doesn't always have the same style, personality, or even profession. However you slice it, she has a fresh and feminine quality that appeals to us like a song we can't get out of our head.

Our favorite semi-modern day flavor of Gwen-TV is not the channel that focuses on the Gwen as sweet, romantic, or mild-mannered. No, we have been drawn to those incarnations of Gwen that mix beautiful with smart (as seen on *The West Wing, Pushing Daisies, Grey's Anatomy, Sex in the City,* and *The Good Wife);* combine the feminine with tough (*Alias, Dollhouse, Firefly, Damages, Veronica Mars,* and the new *Battlestar Gallactica*); and give us heroines who make a habit of saving the world, again and again (*Charmed, Heroes,* and, of course, *Buffy the Vampire Slayer*). Recognizing that many of our examples are from shows that are no longer on the air, we look forward to the next generation of Gwen television stars. She has some big, beautiful, shoes to fill.

Of course, we also prefer the versions of Gwen that remind us that real women are funny as hell (*The Sarah Silverman Program, Adventures of New Christine,* and *30 Rock*).

"So I say we change the rule. I say my power, should be our power...Make your choice. Are you ready to be strong?"[11]

Buffy Summers
Vampire Slayer

"I saw an angel inside the marble and carved until I set him free."

Michelangelo

CHAPTER EIGHT

Super
Sophia

Is There a Little Sophia in You?

☐ I am exactly where I am supposed to be at this moment in time.

☐ I take good care of myself and I know that when I feel good about myself, I can give more honestly to others.

☐ I cleaned out my closet and got rid of all the things that are "not me." It was liberating.

☐ Sure, I've made some mistakes, but I accept them and I keep moving forward.

☐ I have a healthy sense of humor – and it starts with the ability to laugh at myself.

☐ I know what looks good on me, and I've stopped wearing what doesn't. Life's too short to wear acid-wash.

☐ I work toward forgiveness. I have compassion for myself and for others.

☐ I am able to let down my guard and talk about my successes, failures, joys, and pains, creating a safe space that allows others do the same.

☐ Today, I define success by how I treat myself and how I treat others.

☐ I woke up one morning and stopped apologizing for myself. I smile a lot more now.

Who is Sophia?

Sophia is the wise, evolved woman in each of us who knows how to realize her true potential.

Sophia is a superstar. True, it's not as if she landed in the *Guinness Book of World Records*, or made it to the final round of this season's *American Idol*. She hasn't necessarily been on the cover of *In Style* magazine, won a half-dozen Oscars, or rocked-out to a stadium full of screaming fans. Sophia may not have been the company's youngest CEO, received the big promotion or even scored that corner office. But in our book, Sophia has made it. Our Sophia is truly a star: super-cool, super-wise, super-awesome.

     Sophia has found what it is that lights up her life and she practically pulsates with sincere joy. Stand within a five-foot radius of her and you will feel the spark. People can't help but be drawn to her; they are inspired by the world she has created, they sense the ease and the compassion that she has with herself, they get a tingle of the happiness she emanates … and they want a little taste of it. Yes, Sophia has hit the big-time, and for that she has earned a category of status at the end of our journey.

But Sophia is not one to sit on her super-laurels. While she is comfortable in the moment, she knows better than anyone that "making it" is really just one more opportunity to ask, "What's next?" While she honors where she is right now, Sophia loves to challenge herself, play the edge, and take her life to the next level. She knows that just because she is at this story's end, does not for one minute mean that her journey is over. For Sophia, it is always just beginning.

We call Sophia our Wise Woman, but note that this is not a wisdom that she was born with. This is not a wisdom that came from a charm, wish, or a mystical vision. It is not a wisdom that developed overnight. Rather, Sophia is wise in ways that can only come from living, really living. She has seen it all. Felt it all: the good, the bad, the ups, and the downs. She has been around the block more than a few times, experiencing the world and experimenting with her place in it.

After years of second-guessing herself, doing what she thought she was supposed to do and making choices based on playing it safe, Sophia made a new life-changing decision. She decided to stop listening to the noise. She stopped listening to the pesky tapes in her head that kept reminding her of the things she feared and kept putting herself in her own way. She stopped taking comments, suggestions, and advice from the peanut gallery. Sophia refrained from asking the masses, "Do these pants make me look fat?" or "What do you think I should do?" Instead, she turned up the volume on her own intuition and started listening to herself. She found a selective, trusted community of friends with her best interest at heart, and together they help each other get through some pretty tough stuff.

Getting wise to her true self meant rounds and rounds of trial and error: trying and failing, loving and losing, and crashing and burning. Sophia paid her dues, put in a lot of hard work, and has had more than one slip. Each time she falls, she brushes herself off and makes another choice, whether to stay on the current path or forge off on a new one. Through this ongoing process, Sophia has learned who she really is and who she is not, and she has come out smiling.

Take it or leave it. Sophia has stopped apologizing for herself. Where others may see flaws and imperfections, Sophia now sees the quirky parts of her that keep life interesting. She wears her scars like diamonds, holds her head high, and sports a hearty, sincere laugh.

In the end (or is it the beginning?), Sophia is surprised to find that the woman she was looking for has been within her the whole time. She merely has to chip away all that other distracting stuff in order to see her, trust her, and embrace her whole self, bumps and all. If Kate thinks she has to be Superwoman by doing everything; Sophia is wise enough to know that she is super by being everything that she already is.

A funny thing happened when Sophia finally started down this road toward self-acceptance. A shift occurred that opened her up to not only being able to love and accept herself, but also being able to love and accept those around her. What an amazing cycle. Today, Sophia is so sure of her own "super"ness that she easily recognizes and honors the "super" in each of us.

Sophia sees the best in us, sometimes more clearly than we can see it in ourselves. She no longer has to always be right. She doesn't feel the need to tell us what's a little bit wrong with us, point out what imperfection needs a slight tweaking, or give us a mini-course in self-improvement. Instead, she gives us a reassuring nod, acknowledges the depth of who we are, and asks with a smile, "What's next?" She inspires us to grow, push our own boundaries, challenge our perceived limits, and to be gloriously more of who we already are.

Sophia knows we can do it, and she doesn't want us to give up. She knows that this authentic-self business isn't easy. We have to do the work. But she believes in us. Sophia loves where she is and wants us to be there too. She knows there is more than enough room in this crazy world for all of us to be our most super-selves. What a party!

 ## Sophia Values: Radical Self-Acceptance

Sophia has taken the time to figure herself out. Perhaps more importantly, she has figured out how to accept and honor every bit of her super self (even the hard to love parts). Sophia is hopeful that this self-acceptance bug is catching, because she has a grand vision for this world. She doesn't see other people's successes as threatening to her because Sophia knows there is more than enough good to go around. She is secure in her own self and passionate about the life she lives. She is sure the world will be a better place if the rest of us are too.

Sophia's Core Values:

Abundance	*Generosity of Spirit*
Authenticity	*Passion*
Compassion	*Ongoing Self-Awareness*
Dignity	*Transformation*
Empowerment	*Universal Vision*

Perception Is Reality

Sophia has gotten to the point in her life where what you see is what you get. She is comfortable in her own skin and well-rooted in her beliefs. She knows who is she is, what got her here, and where she is going. This might scare the caca out of some of us who aren't quite there yet. All that positive energy and confident self-acceptance can start to rub the most cynical among us the wrong way.

But Sophia does not let the naysayers get into her kitchen. She doesn't want to travel this journey alone, and she knows it can take some time. So, Sophia is patient with us. She knows we'll come around.

Sophia Idealized   Sophia Misunderstood

Sophia Idealized	Sophia Misunderstood
Enjoys her own company	*Lonely*
Happy	*Disingenuous*
Driven by purpose and passion	*Over zealous*
Embraces her own true self	*Vain*
Loves the life she lives	*Irritating*
Stays focused on the present	*Unrealistic*
Gives unconditional love	*Bleeding heart*
Sets and keeps strong boundaries	*Closed off*
The all-knowing wise woman	*The old crone*
Doesn't have to have the last word	*Passive*
Sees the best in others	*Naiive*

When Do You Need Sophia?

Sophia admits that she has not always felt so superwise. Many times in her life she has felt crazy, awkward, and unsure of herself. For years she worried what other people thought about her. She wondered if everyone would notice that she was wearing the wrong shoes for the season, or how long it would take them to find out that she really wasn't smart enough to be in her current position. She was tempted to pencil in, "because I haven't lost the 20 pounds from the second baby yet" when she RSVP'd her regrets to a friend's wedding or to play the "bad hair" card instead of going to the New Year's Eve party. She considered getting a doctor's note for her "condition" of being divorced, single, childless, or just uninterested in the class reunion.

In the end, that was all just a distraction. Transitioning into the self-assured, super self that Sophia is today didn't happen quickly or smoothly. Transformation has its own timetable. There are always new lessons to learn and new experiences to shape and move us. Sophia wants us to be patient, but persistent in this process. Some times the hardest moments are those when we need her most.

Here are some times when we really need a jolt of encouragement from Sophia:

- When you are betrayed by a friend and still have to find room to forgive and love her
- When you need to get out of your own way
- When you need to put yourself in someone else's shoes
- When you hit rock bottom and know you have to keep getting up each day and get out of bed
- When you are shaken by a failure and need to bounce back
- When you need to believe in something bigger
- When your teenage daughter goes on her first date, it is 11:30 p.m. and she is not home yet
- When the invitation to your class reunion comes and you realize that you haven't lost the weight, but you go anyway. You see that no one else is perfect either –

well, except for that one girl named Kate

- When you need someone to tell you that you are more than enough
- When you wake up at 2 am and don't think there is hope and need to figure out a way to talk yourself back to sleep
- When your kids get married and you have to shut up and let them live their own lives
- When you are paralyzed by anxiety and fear and need someone to talk you down
- When your ex-husband comes into town and you baby-sit for your son's kids so they can all go out
- After the job acceptance letter. On your first day. Yes, they made the right decision, get in there
- In the moment – when you have an awesome moment – take the time to recognize it and smile

Sophia *and Her Sisters*

Because she is constantly practicing self-growth and inching towards superstar status, Sophia knows how to take things to the next level. She is the "boost" in our Jamba Juice, the glitch that allows our entry into Mario's "minus world," and the "Bam!" when we need to kick it up notch.

Sophia loves each of the seven women – including herself. Maybe this is because she is so open-minded, but more likely it is because she recognizes herself in each one of them. And she sees each one of us in them too. Sophia sees and honors us in Kate, Zoë, and Donna. She sees and loves us in Hanna, Trudy, and Gwen.

Sophia is encouraged by where each of the seven women is on their own paths. As she has walked with them over the years, she has learned from them. And then, as only Sophia can do, she asked for just a little bit more. More Kate. More Zoë. More Donna. More Hanna. More Trudy. More Gwen. More us!

Before we get to Sophia's own tips, she wants to be sure to share with us what she has drawn out from each of the other women, and what she has been encouraging each one of them to do to continue to raise the universal vibration.

 The secret of Kate's success.

Kate is all about achievement and success. Kate shows us how to get things done, be efficient, stay goal-oriented, and take total responsibility for our lives. From Kate, Sophia is redefining what success looks like. She is able to say, "I am living the kind of life I really want." She knows that having goals and dreams are great motivators for success, but Sophia lives in the now. She holds on to her goals and dreams, but puts her real energy into what is happening in the present … and the dreams, well, they naturally follow.

 Zoë takes a breather.

Zoë shows us how to take time out of our day to breath, to slow down, and smell the patchouli as we head off to our yoga class. Zoë gives us permission to carve out some much-needed time to nurture and take care of ourselves. Sophia loves the idea of self-care, but instead of taking "time out" she has integrated healthy behaviors into her day and her life. She knows that meditation is crucial for her innovation and creativity. Sophia finds the quiet moments throughout the day and it is in those moments that she makes the stronger connection to herself. This in turn connects her more to the world she lives and thrives in.

Donna talks us up.

Donna teaches us to be bold, get noticed and tap into our expertise by developing our personal brand. Donna wants us to speak up, speak out, and have the confidence to sing our own praises and take credit for our accomplishments. Sophia agrees. She not only knows her brand – she lives her brand every day. Her authenticity is clear and her confidence is palatable. She knows who she is and she is clear on who she is not. With such a keen self-awareness she can also see the talents in others. She knows how to build a team around the strengths of others.

 Hanna checks us out.

Or at least she teaches us how to check out. Hanna gives us the okay to unplug, unwind, and sometimes eat the entire bag of Cheetos. Sophia totally gets the rebel spirit in Hanna and understands that detaching a little from the world sometimes actually recharges our creative batteries. Sophia wants us to place more focus on this creative energy, so she encourages us not only to have the periodic day to unplug, but also to stop cramming so much into all those other non-Hanna days. Women are known for their expertise in multitasking. It's our specialty, but Sophia warns that it is distracting us from happiness and actually diminishing our ability to focus. She advises us to stay in the present - be with our kids when we are playing or doing homework. Be with our friends when we are in a conversation instead of answering the phone or sending one quick message from the CrackBerry. Be with your partner – practice active listening and sharing. Be with your parents, at any age; these are the moments that you don't want to check out of.

Trudy is a real-deal change agent.

Trudy embraces diversity and change. Her natural curiosity allows her to be open to adventure as she explores all things new and shiny. Sophia takes Trudy's ability to change and grow to new depths. The deeper that Sophia goes in true acceptance of herself, the more real she becomes.

Being open to seeing things in a new way is a necessary part of a long-lasting transformation of self. The beauty of this powerful self-transformation is that it is like alchemy: when you mix truths together there is a deep and lasting change that doesn't morph back. Oh, but you can always add more to the mix…and the process continues, ever expanding.

 Gwen is our natural woman.

Gwen embodies the female spirit. She is feminine to the core and is not afraid to show it. Sophia cheers Gwen on and is the female leader fully realized. She leads with her heart and urges Gwen, and all of us, to do the same. Sophia sees the world changing and recognizes Gwen's place in it. She sees a new generation of women leaders working in a collaborative way to find innovative, creative solutions to address the complex problems of our age. It is time for men and women alike to come together – to celebrate our commonalities and our differences, and strive for new relationship models at work, in our communities and in our homes.

Top 10 Tips *from Sophia*
for happiness now!

Sophia recently read a study on women and happiness and it made her a little sad. The research concluded that women are not as happy as they were 40 years ago, while men are getting a little happier. Betsey Stevenson and Justin Wolfer's research, "The Paradox of Declining Female Happiness," suggests that even though the lives of women have considerably improved over the last 35 years their happiness has declined.

There seems to be a disconnection. After all, women today are generally more independent, wealthier, better educated, and healthier than they were 40 years ago. Women around the world are running governments as powerful as Germany and companies as large as Pepsi. Today women are empowered to live their best lives (thank you Oprah, er, Sophia). Women play competitive sports, join the armed forces, play guitars, and ride Harleys. Today women outnumber men enrolled in universities as well as in the workforce. How can we not be happy?

Sophia finds this hard to swallow, but she gets it. She has been there herself and she does not try to belittle what women are feeling or try to negate those very real feelings. Sophia does not pretend to have the secret to happiness, but she does, however, want to share a few things that she has learned along her own path that have made her feel, well, happier, and ever more grateful.

1. *Don't wait to be happy.* There's no time like the present. In life, most days are pretty average. Then every once in a while a great moment creeps in and we take notice. These "Cloud Nine" moments evoke a strong positive emotion in us, so stop and let yourself feel what you feel. Revel in your moment whether it comes after having a hard conversation with a friend, seeing your baby take her first step, getting some well-deserved recognition from your boss, or even taking a walk with your aging dad. Most of the time these are not planned events. They are simple things that happen from time to time and make you feel good about yourself and your life. And in those moments that is as good as it gets.

2. *Act "As If."* Sophia learned this tip from Jack Canfield, the *Chicken Soup* guru. Give it a try. Jack tells us to act as if you are happy, as if you are living the life you want. Act as if you are fun, smart, and beautiful and somehow acting as if tell your mind you are! The old "Fake it till you make it" holds a lot of truth. Stop saying things like, "I'll be happy when ____" or "if only I could ____." The trick is to smile and act as if you are happy. Practice smiling and laughing, and soon your brain gets the important message, "Hey! I am happy."

3. *Perform daily random acts of kindness.* According to a report in *Time* magazine, doing good deeds can boost your happiness. Who knew? The concept goes something like this: many of us have negative thoughts about ourselves dancing around in our heads. Whether we call it low self-esteem, self-loathing, or the inability to truly love one's self, many of us do not believe that we are nice, kind, or generous. By simply performing random acts of kindness on a daily basis we actually trick our brains into liking us and thinking good thoughts about ourselves. If we do random acts of kindness on a daily basis soon we start smiling more and benefit from an overall hit of self-love.

People may even begin to smile at work and do nice things for each other.

4. *Write thank-you notes.* It may seem simple, but saying a little "thank you" can go a long way. If you are not into seeing the glass-half-full, this exercise may be able to help you. Start by writing a couple of thank-you notes each evening before you go to sleep. It is a sure way to get you ready for a soothing and peaceful night's sleep. Dr. Roizen, Oprah's star medical man and director of the Cleveland Clinic Wellness Program, revealed that he writes two thank you notes each evening before going to bed. It is a ritual that he has integrated into his life that helps him end his day in gratitude. He says that the simple act of writing a gratitude note may help you feel more enthusiastic and positive, plus it's always nice to give a nod to those who helped you get where you are.

5. *See the good.* Practice self-acceptance. Self-acceptance allows us to cut ourselves some slack. It is all about awareness of our strengths as well as our weaknesses, and being OK with both. Self-acceptance alleviates the constant pressure to improve or "fix" our flaws. Instead, we start from a place of seeing and honoring the good in ourselves and others. We stop saying, "I know. I'm so bad. I'm working on that." Once we admit that it is perfectly fine not to be "perfect" then any refinements we make are just beautiful enhancements to something that is already beautiful. Playing our edge, challenging ourselves, pushing ourselves to stretch and grow is not about fixing ourselves or making our bad selves better, but about making something that is already pretty darn great, even more so.

6. *Have a good laugh at YOU.* Stop taking everything so seriously. Having the ability to see the humor in our actions helps. As acclaimed stress expert Loretta Laroche says, "One of the most divine things you can encroach upon is the concept that you are the joke."[12] If you don't believe it, then just ask Kathy Griffin from *My Life on the D List.*

7. *Play big.* Do more of what you really want to do. If you like to sing, sing it from the rooftop. If you like to hike, get out to the mountains. If you like gardening, really go green! Don't just start with a few tulips. Get into it and plant an entire barrel of tulips. You will be happy that you put the time into it come next spring. Go a little deeper with things. It's about figuring out what you want to do and doing it. A lot of people talk about what they would do if they could. Sophia just does it.

8. *Set some boundaries.* Avoid the Hoovers. Hoovers are the people who suck out all of your joy and energy. Hoovers fall into the negative, complaining, victim category. They see the glass half empty and spill the rest. As much as Sophia is committed to helping folks draw out their true potential, she learned early on to avoid spending too much energy on Hoovers. Don't get drawn into their drama. Take stock of all aspects of your life and ask yourself which ones are working and which ones need more focus. Let go of the people that are robbing you of joy and purpose.

9. *Break a few rules.* Sophia admits that she is not confined by rules. Sometimes you have to look the other way in order to get things done! She learned early in her life not to be locked into to the way things are always done but rather how thing can be done. Sure, she' a risk-taker, and at times she runs the risk of being wrong in her attempt to get things done. That's the downside to living on the edge.

10. *We strengthen ourselves by strengthening others.* Be a teacher and mentor to others. Learning starts with listening and asking good questions. As we listen to others we are learning, reflecting, assimilating and then teaching by implementing a plan that incorporates others ideas. To learn you have to keep asking questions.

"I want history to remember me not just as the first black woman to be elected to Congress, not as the first black woman to have made a bid for the presidency of the United States, but as a black woman who lived in the 20th century and dared to be herself."

Shirley Chisholm

Dressing *with Sophia*
Sophia knows what works for her.

Because Sophia has such a strong sense of self and body-awareness, her style is individualistic and very much her own. She takes the "best of" suggestions from the other six women, and uses what works best for her. Doing this, she has built a wardrobe full of items that reflect who she really is. She recommends that we go back and look through the closets of the other women and do the same for ourselves.

But Sophia does have one last wardrobe tip for us, and that is about the art of collecting jewelry, accessories and distinctive pieces that show off who you are and have special meaning to you. She encourages you to seek out clothing lines and jewelry designers that bring out the truest expression of your best self.

 ## Famous Sophias:

Do you recognize Sophia in any of these wise women?

Alice Walker	*J.K. Rolins*
Anne Lamott	*Toni Morrison*
Annie Leibovitz	*Michelle Obama*
Susan Sarandon	*Maya Angelou*
Mary J. Blige	*Marianne Williamson*
Elizabeth Gilbert	*Meryl Streep*
Sheryl Crow	*Arianna Huffington*
Salma Hayek	*Oprah*
Isabel Allende	*Queen Rania of Jordan*
Julie Andrews	*Toni Morrison*
Jamie Lee Curtis	*Gloria Steinem*

Sophia's Bookshelf

- *Find Your Strongest Life: What the Happiest and Most Successful Women Do Differently,* by Marcus Buckingham
- *Emotional Freedom: Liberate Yourself from Negative Emotions and Transform Your Life,* by Judith Orloff, M.D.
- *Bluebird: Women and the New Psychology of Happiness,* by Ariel Gore
- *The Spiritual Anatomy of Emotion: How Feelings Link the Brain, the Body, and the Sixth Sense,* by Michael A. Jawer and Marc S. Micozzi, M.D., Ph.D.
- *Influencer- the Power to Change Anything,* by Patterson, Greeny, Mayfield, McMillan, Switzer
- *Radical Self-Acceptance: Embracing Your Life with the Heart of a Buddha,* by Tara Brach
- *Something More,* by Sarah Ban Breathnach
- *On Becoming Fearless,* by Arianna Huffington

Movies On Sophia's Netflix Queue

Angles in America	*Out of Africa*
Field of Dreams	*The Blind Side*
Heaven Can Wait	*A League of Their Own*
Julie and Julia	*Fried Green Tomatoes*
Joy Luck Club	*The Color Purple*
Erin Brockovich	*Men Don't Leave*
Life is Beautiful	*It's Complicated*
Mamma Mia!	*Something's Gotta Give*
Volver	*Prince of Tides*
Terms of Endearment	*Under the Tuscan Sun*

What's *Next?*

As she gazes into her crystal ball, Sophia can see the spectrum of all women past, present and future – the map of where we've been to and where we need to go, and she's open to the changes ahead.

Sophia thanks the women who came before her - her mother and her mother's mother, and all the others who cleared the way and softened the journey for her. She values the lessons learned from these strong women and from those whom she is fortunate enough to have in her community now.

She earnestly passes on her own wisdom, and can't wait to see what is still to come from the creative new female leaders of today who are shaking things up as they lead the way along this great adventure.

"Happiness is the consequence of personal effort. You fight for it, strive for it, insist upon it, and sometimes even travel around the world looking for it. You have to participate relentlessly in the manifestations of your own blessings. And once you have achieved a state of happiness, you must never become lax about maintaining it. You must make a mighty effort to keep swimming upward into that happiness forever, to stay afloat on top of it." [13]

Elizabeth Gilbert
Eat, Pray, Love

"We begin to find and become ourselves when we notice how we are already found, already truly, entirely, wildly, messily, marvelously who we were born to be."[14]

Anne Lamott

EPILOGUE

When we started working on *The Seven Women Project* 10 years ago, we had no idea what was on the horizon. In the decade that this book has been in development, much has changed – in our lives, our country and our world. We could probably go as far as suggest that this has been a time of unprecedented change…and that we are all really holding on for the ride.

As authors we have experienced personal change: changes in direction and in career, moves to new homes, and entrance into new communities. We have welcomed new friends, new business associates, and even new family members. And while the Girls Scouts sing, "make new friends but keep the old," sadly some of this change has also come with loss and, we would be lying if we failed to mention, sadness. But through this decade of rather intense self-reflection, we have also seen amazing personal growth and, dare we say it, transformation.

More broadly, in our country and in our world, the past decade has clearly been one marked by change of all kinds – in security, the economy, technology, weather patterns, politics, social policy, and the environment to name just a few. Some change has been exciting, but quite a bit of it has been scary, shocking, and in some cases quite devastating.

Yes, we are living through dynamic times that are both inspiring and troubling, often in the same moment.

In the face of such dramatic change we know how easy it is to get discouraged, disappointed, and overwhelmed. It is not hard to feel small and insignificant. And we would never want to discount these very real feelings. But we have also seen that in the face of such unprecedented change, in addition to some big hurdles, there are also big opportunities. And we have continued to meet women and men over the past decade who have challenged us to see that it is really how we face these changes that matters.

We have come to realize that we are not facing any of this alone, and we believe that as women it is vital that we encourage, support, and elevate other. We believe that through our daily contributions, interactions, and relationships we can begin to make a magnificent difference in our families, our communities, and our world.

The Seven Women Project is our humble contribution to the cause. It is an offering we make in gratitude because we believe in women, and we believe in you. We add our playful voice to this much grander dialogue as a way to say that we believe that you are not small, you are not insignificant, you are not "less than" – you are enough. Really, you are more than enough. And we want to see more of you. More of your inner awareness, self-confidence, creativity, youthful open-mindedness, feminine spirit, and wisdom. Bring it!

We have given voice to the seven extraordinary women that we have seen in women around the world. But we want to hear who else is in there. What other women are inside you? What are their names? What are they like? How do they help you bring out and share with the world aspects of your most amazing and authentic self?

The Seven Women Project is about women, and it is about us. This is a story about being connected to ourselves and to those around us. And it is a story that continues to evolve and grow. We invite you to evolve and grow with us, and to have a great time out there changing the world.

Keep in touch,

Karen and Meredith
www.thesevenwomenproject.com

"You are the storyteller of your own life,
and you can create your own legend or not."

Isabel Allende

ACKNOWLEDGEMENTS

The Seven Women Project grew out of our mother-daughter partnership, but each of the women in the book has become more real, more vibrant, and more alive through a much larger network of collaboration. Friends have added to our work by sharing their thoughts on the women and how they relate to each of them. Family members have chimed in. Women attending Karen's programs have provided feedback. Sometimes it seems that near strangers on the street have stopped us to share stories from their own experiences, but we could be imagining that.

The truth is *The Seven Women Project* could not have gone from concept to reality without the help, input, and support of so many wonderful people: women and men. And we are ever grateful. This is our honest attempt to publicly thank as many of our contributors as we can. Of course, if we have inadvertently left someone out, please accept our deep apologies and know that we thank you too!

Fabulous Family

We are blessed to have a talented and generous extended family that has not only supported us along the way, but is also an integral part of our team.

Mike Svat, nephew/cousin, is our Creative Director (read Creative Genius), who produced our cover art and photography, designed and managed the page layout, and endured multiple rounds of a grueling tweaking process. We couldn't have done this without you!

Ben McCullough, son/brother, is the brains behind the website and blog for *The Seven Women Project*. He took our ideas and created a great design that we can't wait to continue to grow into. He has also done his best to try to keep us "fair and balanced." Loving thanks also to Ben's beautiful family, his wife Sarah and the twins Campbell and Connally (Happy First Birthday girls, this one is for you).

Terry Svat and Pat Fischer, sisters/aunts, these two fantastic, fiery women kept Karen on her toes. And their morning phone calls encouraged Karen and motivated her to get going. Not to mention Terry's painstaking, line-by-line reading of an early draft resulted in some great catches and new ideas. Thanks to their husbands too, Jerry and Ray, respectively.

Speaking of great catches, Megan Paris Rundlet, a great married-in addition to our family, also did a detailed read-through and shared her thoughts with us. Thanks!

We would be remiss not to mention the rest of "the cousins," many of whom were the same ones who came to Houston to help with "the store" in Chapter 1. Thank goodness they stuck around and continue to bring joy and laughter into our lives. They are: Kim Healy and her husband James; Marybeth Wuenschel and her husband Mark; Chris Fischer and his wife Kelly; Judi Fischer Klausmeyer and her husband Kurt; Rhea Shoop and her husband Charlie; and Laura Svat Rundlet and her husband Peter.

Of course, they are also directly responsible for "the kids table" including: Chris, Hanna (inspired the naming of one of our women, but insists the chapter is not based on her), Faith, Peter, David, Michael, Rachel, Brooke, Barbara, Jacob, Anna, Jonathan, Emme, Sabine, August and Elise. Thanks for keeping us young. You all rock!

Thank you also to Meredith's dad, Bruce McCullough, and his family, especially the voracious reader, Amanda Bard. We hope this makes it to your bookshelf.

We would also like to thank Meredith's partner, James T. Whitcomb, for all his encouragement and for keeping a sense of humor even during the never-ending "crunch time." That's right, he's not from Texas, but we think the T stands for "totally awesome." He was one of the first in Meredith's circle to start addressing this book as something that would actually be published, rather than just a far-off dream. Thanks Jamie!

Finally, we mentioned our beloved Rose Speranza in the dedication. We would also like to thank her husband, our father and grandfather who is still cheering us on at 103 years old. As Mike says, "Are you having any fun? God love ya!"

Amazing Artists and Excellent Editors

In addition to our family members mentioned above. There are a number of individuals who also helped to make this book shine.

Shyama Golden, Gen Y artist and graphic designer from Austin, literally gave our women faces, (long!) legs, and great style. She breathed life into each woman with the stroke of her brush.

A special thank you to Susan Howard who read and edited an early draft of the book. She helped us get over a hump that could have delayed the project indefinitely. She also encouraged Meredith to add her voice and speak up to be part of "Karen's Story."

Thanks also to Julie Anderson (aka "Comma Queen") for reading one of the last versions of the text, and combing through it one last time. Phew!

There is also a whole group of women and men who read the advanced copy of the book and provided their edit marks, comments, cheers, and even testimonials. Thanks to you all, in no particular order: Amy Ippoliti, Katherine Osborne Valdez, Julie Haralson, Kerry McBride, Bambi McCullough, Karen Davis, Cecilia Rose, Lisa Journagan, Debbie Allen, Andrea Evers, Laura McCreary, Teri Battaglieri, Laura Lopez, Malissa McLeod, Desirée Rumbaugh, Ren Resch, Donna Fisher, Kim Zeiner, Garrison Wynn, Aurelie Gallagher Krauss, Connie Podesta, and Beverly Denver.

We are truly grateful to everyone who had a hand in editing this work. If any inconsistencies or questionable grammar remain, you are off the hook – we claim these as ours alone!

Our Creative Communities

We acknowledge that we would not be where we are today if we weren't part of something bigger than the both of us. We are grateful to the communities that sustain us and we hope that our work is part of a grand conversation that continues to raise all of us up, and up, and up.

Karen would like to say thank you to the National Speakers Associate (NSA) – both the local Houston Chapter and all the great speakers across the nation. Thank you in particular to Linda Talley,

Tom Britton, Theresa Behenna, Jim Bob Solsbery, Ann Perle, and Jill Hickman. You are all superstars.

She also gives thanks to The Professional Group (TPG), a breakfast club. Thanks to Callie Shields, Maureen Sanders, Trish Rumble, and everyone in the TPG crew.

Of course, weekday nights and Sundays at 4:30 p.m. wouldn't be the same in the Houston Heights, without Shannon, Mike, Amonia', Lovely, and Jazzercise Jane. Thanks Jane for getting Karen's inner-Hanna out of the house and into the groove.

Karen is also grateful for the long-time support of her friends and colleagues in Houston, particularly retailer Bev Po-erschke, photographer Tracey Rubio, and Cindy Brown. And in Cleveland – thank you, Mary Brown.

For her part, Meredith would like to give a shout-out to her Texas posse, including the Grad School Gurus and Team ACL. Thanks to you crazy kids for keeping the creative juices flowing and rocking her world. Again in no particular order thanks to Rachel Poynter, Amy Fauver, Elissa Steglich, Stephanie Luongo, Lorie Eberly, Dawn Hagan, Kathy Miller, Kristin Keeling, and John "Johnny Cam" Shultzabarger who has been listening to her talk about "the book" for a long, long time. Of course, she also has special admiration for the Road Warriors who kept her sane during her days as a traveling consultant. Thanks to Heidi Burbage, Larissa "Diva" Lamson, and "the Rays," especially Ray Eldredge.

Meredith would also like to thank the yoga *kula* (community) in Washington DC, Houston, Denver, and across the country. These folks keep her inspired and constantly striving to raise the vibration. Thanks to the excellent instructors and friends at MINT, Willow Street Yoga, and Spiral Flight Yoga. Special thanks to Kelly Griswold, Naomi Gottlieb-Miller, and Alexis Britton who first introduced her to the world of Anusara yoga. And thanks again Amy and Des. Bird it.

Finally, Meredith would like to thank Annie Cahill Kelly, Scott Curtis, and Katie Bergin who volunteered with her in Chile. Preparing for this two-year adventure, Katie and Meredith struggled with packing for a range of possible situations; we threw in a skirt or two because "you can't be Hiker Girl all the time." Who knew? Special thanks also to the women of Chile, including Sara,

Angelica, and Soledad, who first opened Meredith's eyes to the beauty, strength and general wonderfulness of women. Gracias.

And how could we forget...

We would like to thank all the "real women on the runway," the models and audience that helped get the early *The Seven Women Project* runway shows off the ground. You are too many to name, but we would like to mention Melanie Stewart, Pam Bacinich, J-Bird Cook, Valerie Praitor, Nancy Hopper, Suzanne Penley, Mary Denny, Diana Huntress, Firoozh Tuller, Deniese Sadberry, Jane Luco, and many more.

Similarly, we offer loads of gratitude to the ladies who worked and shopped at Me Too...Me Too... In addition to the family, thanks to Jennifer Kitzmiller McMahon, Karen Ledbetter, and Frenchi Boydon. You became family. Thank you.

There are a couple people out there that don't even know they helped. As we navigated our way through the world of self-publishing, we relied upon the words and advice from folks like Sam Horn, Debra Fine, Nancy Nichols, Steve Weber, and Dan Poynter.

One last note

Throughout the book we mention a number of stores, clothing and jewelry lines, music, movies, web sites, and other products. We did this for one simple reason – it's stuff we like, or that we think one of our women would like. Please note that we did not get paid for these mentions. We believe in the power of abundance, and we are big fans of promoting the people and things that we enjoy.

If *The Seven Women Project* is something that you enjoy, spread the word. And then get back to us. Send us an email or comment on the website or blog. Send us a snail mail postcard. Friend us! We want to hear from you.

And a big thank you to each of you.

Notes and Copyright Notices

[1] Page 15. Williamson, Marianne. *A Return to Love: Reflections on the Principles of a Course in Miracles.* Harper Collins, 1992.

[2] Page 32. Myers Briggs refers to a widely used personality assessment instrument developed by Katherine Cooks Briggs and Isabel Briggs in the 1940s.

[3] Page 37. Podesta,Connie. *Make a Fortune Selling to Women: The Deal Makers and Deal Breakers You Must Know to Close the Deal Every Time.* Greenleaf Book Group Press, 2009.

[4] Page 58. Ban Breath, Sarah. *Simple Abundance: A Daybook of Comfort and Joy.* Warner Books, Inc., 1995.

[5] Page 69-70. Ban Breath,Sarah. *Simple Abundance: Journal of Gratitude.* Grand Central Publishing, 1996.

[6] Page 87. Comaford-Lynch, Christine. *Rules for Renegades: How to Make More Money, Rock your Career, and Revel in Your Individuality.* McGraw-Hill, 2007.

[7] Page 90. Klaus, Peggy. *Brag! The Art of Tooting Your Own Horn without Blowing It.* Warner Books Inc., 2003.

[8] Page 106. *Sex and the City*, Series on HBO, 1998 – 2004. Episode "My Motherboard, Myself," July 15, 2001. Darren Star (creator), Candace Bushnell (book), Julie Rottenberg (screenplay), Elisa Zuritsky (screenplay)

[9] Page 124. *30 Rock*, Series on NBC. Episode "Black Light Attack!" January 14, 2010. Tina Fey (creator), Steve Hely (writer).

[10] Page 127. Did you guess what trends are associated with each of our famous Trudys? Here are the answers:

Beyonce – leotards
Katie Holmes – the bob haircut
Jennifer Aniston – defining hair styles
Farrah Fawcett – the wings
Meg Ryan – bed-head hair
Rihanna – pixie haircut
Gwen Stefani – rocker chic
Cameron Diaz – the one-shoulder look
Sienna Miller – boho chic / the total groove
Sarah Jessica Parker – Manolos and more
Mary Kate Olsen – the bag lady look
Carla Bruni Sarkozy – ballet flats
Diane Keaton – menswear chic
Anne Hathaway – red lips
Madonna – fingerless gloves, crucifixes, leg warmers, and so much more!

[11] Page 155. *Buffy the Vampire Slayer*, Series by Mutant Enemy on the WB and UPN, 1997-2003. Episode "Chosen," May 20, 2003. Joss Whedon (creator & writer).

[12] Page 172. LaRoche, Loretta. *The Best of Loretta LaRoche.* (audio CD) Hay House, 2004.

[13] Page 176. Gilbert, Elizabeth. *Eat, Pray, Love: One Woman's Search for Everything Across Italy, India and Indonesia.* Penguin Group, 2006.

[14] Page 178. Lamott, Anne. "Becoming the Person You Were Meant to Be." *O, The Oprah Magazine,* October, 2009.

THE AUTHORS

The Seven Women Project was born out of personal observation, interaction and a whole lot of creative fun. We do not claim to be psychologists or personality experts. We are a mother-daughter team. Together we run the gamut as: a motivational speaker and a government consultant; a business owner and an international volunteer; a jazzercise fanatic and a yoga instructor. We are a dog-walker and a marathon runner; fashionista and feminista; the cool kid and the pop-culture nerd; a Baby Boomer and a Gen X'er... And the mere fact that we have completed this 10-year project without killing each other is a feat unto itself.

Karen McCullough is a nationally known keynote speaker, and it's been said that she is the most fun you'll ever have while learning! Through her study of human behavior, workplace trends, and branding, Karen has developed an innovative approach to connecting with audiences as she integrates the business, personal, and cultural aspects of life. For over 20 years, Karen was a CEO and buyer for several fashion retail stores in Houston, Texas. Today Karen energizes women's groups, business leaders, and employees across the country. Her programs provide both men and women with tools they need to improve productivity, take concrete action, and make changes necessary to achieve the success they desire, no matter their age or position.

Meredith McCullough is a full-time technology and policy consultant, who has always been drawn to working with women and building community. After graduation from Norte Dame she spent two years running women's groups Santiago, Chile and did graduate work at the University of Texas at Austin in women's political participation. With over 15 years of experience and training in project management and program development, she has worked with international agencies, state and local organizations, and most recently, the Federal government. It is her dedication to teaching yoga, her passion for empowering women of all ages, and her love of pop-culture that really gets Meredith excited about life. At the end of the day, Meredith is, at heart, her mother's daughter.

Illustrator *Shyama Golden's* first love has always been drawing, but her training in graphic design has always been a major influence on her art. Fashion illustration has been her hobby since childhood and she has a background in the publishing industry as well as in interactive design. She now runs her own design and illustration firm with clients of all sizes, from Fortune 500 to startups. Her work strives to reward the viewer who looks closely with an unexpected layer of detail or humor. She works in a variety of media, often combining the handmade with technology. Her illustrations have appeared in nationally recognized magazines across the country

Quick Order Form

Order the Seven Women Project for your next conference, retreat, training or any event that includes women!

Quantity pricing for direct purchase or sponsorship of the book All discounts are savings from the retail price of $17.95.

25 - 100	$15.00 ea.
101 - 250	$14.00 ea.
251 - 499	$13.00 ea.
500 - 1000	$10.00 ea.
1000+	$9.00 ea.

Call for a pricing proposal or an estimate to your location. Prices do not include freight and handling.

(713) 880-8784 or (832) 687-1051

Call or Email

info@thesevenwomenproject.com

Please send me _____ books.

Name: _____

Address: _____

City: _____ *State:* _____

Zip Code: _____

Telephone: _____

Email address: _____

Fax Order to: *(713) 880-0414*   **Attn:** *Michael Svat*

Mail Order to: *Michael Svat*
                    1302 Waugh Dr. #344
                    Houston, TX 77019

Join the Seven Women discussion on our website & blog:
www.thesevenwomenproject.com